Simply Serving

Recipes from the Heart of Texas

Junior League of Waco, Inc.

The Junior League is indebted to

Community Bank & Trust as the main sponsor

for this cookbook project.

Founded in 1952, family-owned and operated,

Community Bank & Trust is enthusiastic about Waco and

has always been supportive of the League's projects.

Simply Serving

Recipes from the Heart of Texas

Junior League of Waco, Inc.

Simply Serving
Recipes from the Heart of Texas

Published by the Junior League of Waco, Inc.

Copyright © 2005
The Junior League of Waco, Inc.
2600 Austin Avenue
Waco, Texas 76710
254-753-5574

Food Photography: © Joe Griffin
Food Stylist: Loren Lee

Library of Congress Catalog Number: 2005926737
ISBN: 0-9768116-0-X

Edited, Designed, and Manufactured by
Favorite Recipes® Press
an imprint of

FRP

P. O. Box 305142
Nashville, Tennessee 37230
800-358-0560

Art Director: Steve Newman
Book Design: Starletta Polster
Project Manager and Editor: Jane Hinshaw

Printed in China
First Printing 2005
10,000 copies

From the Presidents

The Junior League of Waco was founded in 1935 by a group of Waco women who recognized the need to promote community service through voluntarism, to develop the potential of women, and to improve the quality of life for McLennan County families.

That was 69 years ago, and in 2005-2006, we will celebrate 70 years of volunteer service!

The League is one of the largest volunteer-driven, nonprofit organizations in our community, and has a rich history of researching and identifying community needs, determining how best to meet these recognized needs and, in the process, making a significant difference in the lives of children and their families.

Our projects are identified and selected based on our mission of sharing a common vision and our commitment to improving the quality of life for families in our community. We are committed to improving the physical, intellectual, and emotional development of children and adolescents in McLennan County.

Since 1935, the Junior League of Waco has invested millions of dollars in our community through projects, grants, and volunteer training. These financial contributions, paired with hours of volunteer service to area nonprofit agencies and schools, continue a League legacy of positive and significant change in our home community.

Simply Serving: Recipes from the Heart of Texas continues the rich tradition originated with the publication of our first cookbook, *Hearts and Flours,* and showcases our history of service to this community.

We simply want to thank you. By purchasing this book, you are supporting the community projects of the Junior League of Waco and making an investment in the lives of many. Our hope is that you not only enjoy these recipes, but also view the Junior League and our community through new eyes—and taste buds!

Kathy McCarty Douthit　　　　　　*Angela Eads Tekell*
President 2004-2005　　　　　　President 2005-2006

Contents

Acknowledgments 8

Introduction 9

Menus 10

Appetizers & Beverages 18

Soups & Salads & Sandwiches 46

Main Dishes 68

Side Dishes 110

Breads & Breakfast & Brunch 124

Desserts 146

Family-Friendly Fare 176

Celebrated Chefs & Restaurants 194

Contributors 214
Index 216
Order Information 223

Acknowledgments

Thanks to photographer Joe Griffin, owner of Griffin Photography for 28 years. He has been published in *Newsweek, Moody Monthly,* and *Texas Monthly,* and has won awards for both his commercial images and portraits.

Thanks to Loren Lee, chef and owner of Mirth, for preparing the recipes pictured in the book. Her expertise and style were invaluable to our success.

Thanks to Kim Olsen of Flowers by Design for lending her creativity and donating the floral arrangements for our photographs. Her signature style and unique flair paired beautifully with the culinary creations.

Cookbook Development Committee

Melissa Cates — *Co-Chair*
Mandy Kuehl — *Co-Chair*
Lori Lutz — *Marketing Chair*
Ali Abercrombie — *Nonrecipe Text Co-Chair*
Gretchen Eichenberg — *Nonrecipe Text Co-Chair*
Leandra Wash-Cole — *Art and Design Chair*
Debbie Wooley — *Recipe Chair*

Committee Members
JoAn Felton
Leslie Horne
Erica McKay

Sustainer Advisors
Jennifer Heinz
Docia Lawless
Ellie Morrison
Carol Sedberry
Lauri Smith
Barbara Williamson

Introduction

Welcome to the heart of Texas, where serving others is simply a part of life. From a simple meal for family to a special menu for your supper club, the act of preparing and serving a meal for another speaks louder and clearer than most words. Whether offering guests a loaf of home-baked bread or delicious shellfish crepes, the hospitality extended is just as important as the food on the table.

The Junior League of Waco invites you to dine with us as we present *Simply Serving: Recipes from the Heart of Texas.* We hope this cookbook will inspire you to bring family and friends together to enjoy exceptional meals, as well as each other.

In seventy years of service, the Junior League of Waco has brought to the table many of the resources and trained volunteers needed to improve the quality of life for families in our community. Your purchase of *Simply Serving* enables the Junior League of Waco to continue in these efforts through our numerous community projects.

Simply Serving: Recipes from the Heart of Texas is not our League's first cookbook. *Hearts and Flours,* published in 1988, has brought much joy into the kitchens and homes of Wacoans and others over the years. Though now out of print, our League still receives requests for *Hearts and Flours.* So, we've included in this book some time-honored recipes in an Heirloom Collection. Thank you to the *Hearts and Flours* cookbook committee, who paved the way for us.

Time may seem scarce today, but good food doesn't have to be, and it's always worth serving. Remember that what you bring to the table isn't as important as what you put into it, who you share it with, or the act of *simply serving* it.

 Designates Heirloom Collection Recipes

Bright & Early Brunch

Fresh Fruit with Sweet Cream Dip

Brunch Casserole

Lemon-Glazed Zucchini Pecan Bread

Cheese Danish

Strawberry Banana Punch

Menu

Let's Do Lunch

Tomato Basil Soup with Cheese Petits Fours

Grape Salad

Wild Rice and Tuna Salad

Rosemary Cookies

Almond Tea

Game Day Goodies

Oyster Crackers

Stuffed Jalapeños

Cowboy Caviar with Corn Chips

Tailgate Sandwiches

Fall Popcorn Balls

Pecan Bars

Backyard Barbecue

Better Cheddar Spread

Crunchy Asian Slaw

Barbecued Dove

Cheesy Potato Casserole

Brazos Baked Beans

One-Hour Rolls

Milky Way Ice Cream

Menu

Enjoy a Little Italy

Olive and Cheese Crostini

Sunflower Spinach Salad

Spaghetti Carbonara

Focaccia

Crème de Menthe Parfaits

Menu

Viva de Mexico

Salsa Verde with Tortilla Chips

Mini Mexican Shells

Sour Cream Chicken Enchiladas

Cilantro and Lime Rice

Beans à la Chara

Caramel Dumplings

Sangria

Menu

Serving Up Supper Club

Sweet Baked Brie with Chipotle Peach Sauce

Butter Lettuce Salad with Pomegranate Vinaigrette

Jalapeño-Stuffed Pork Tenderloin

Sweet Carrot Soufflé

Asparagus Risotto

Home-Baked Yeast Bread

Rum Cake

Menu

Dinner Divine

Blue Cheese Asparagus Rolls

Roasted Mushroom Salad

Shellfish Crepes in Wine Cheese Sauce

Crème Brûlée

Chocolate Martini

Appetizers & Beverages

Get things going with a savory dip;

Serve up a drink that's sparkling and hip.

Once guests arrive and fill up the space,

The rest of the meal will fall right into place.

This chapter graciously underwritten by Waco Coca-Cola Bottling Company

Sweet Baked Brie

1 round of Brie cheese
2 tablespoons butter, softened
1/4 to 1/2 cup packed brown sugar
slivered almonds or pecans (optional)

Preheat the oven to 325 degrees. Slice off the top rind of the cheese and score the top of the cheese. Mix the butter and brown sugar in a bowl.

Place the cheese in a small baking dish and top with the brown sugar mixture; sprinkle with almonds. Bake for 15 minutes or until the cheese is soft and the topping is bubbly. Serve with French bread. You can also top the cheese with Chipotle Peach Sauce (below).

Serves 8

Chipotle Peach Sauce

1/4 cup apple cider vinegar
1/4 cup water
2 piloncillo cones, or 6 ounces dark brown sugar
juice of 2 limes
1 to 3 dried chipotle chiles, crushed
5 peaches, peeled and sliced
1 teaspoon kosher salt

Combine the vinegar, water, piloncillo cones, lime juice, chipotle chiles, peaches and salt in a saucepan and mix well. Bring to a boil, stirring to dissolve the cones. Adjust the heat to medium-high and cook for 20 minutes, stirring occasionally.

Store in an airtight container in the refrigerator for several weeks. Use to top Brie cheese or serve with pork or poultry.

Makes 1 1/2 cups

Blue Cheese Asparagus Rolls

20 asparagus spears
4 ounces blue cheese, softened
8 ounces cream cheese, softened

1 egg, beaten
20 thin slices white bread
1 cup (2 sticks) butter, melted

Steam the asparagus until tender-crisp. Combine the blue cheese, cream cheese and egg in a bowl and mix until smooth. Trim the crusts from the bread and roll flat with a rolling pin.

Spread the cheese mixture on the bread and arrange 1 asparagus spear diagonally on each slice. Roll the bread to enclose the asparagus and secure with a wooden pick. Dip in the butter, coating well. Place on a baking sheet and freeze until firm.

Preheat the oven to 400 degrees. Slice each asparagus roll into 3 pieces. Bake for 15 minutes or until brown.

Serves 20

Chicken Curry Bites

24 unbaked miniature puff pastry shells
1 pound boneless skinless
   chicken breasts
1 cup (4 ounces) shredded Swiss cheese
1 (8-ounce) can water chestnuts,
   drained and chopped

2 tablespoons chopped scallions
1/2 to 1 cup mayonnaise
1 teaspoon lemon juice
1 teaspoon curry powder
6 tablespoons cranberry chutney

Bake the pastry shells using the package directions. Combine the chicken with enough water to cover in a saucepan and cook until tender. Drain the chicken and chop into small pieces.

Preheat the oven to 400 degrees. Combine the chicken with the Swiss cheese, water chestnuts, scallions, mayonnaise, lemon juice and curry powder in a large bowl; mix well. Spoon into the baked pastry shells and top with the chutney. Place on a baking sheet and bake for 10 minutes. Serve hot.

Makes 24

Bacon-Wrapped Chicken Bites

1/4 cup soy sauce
2 tablespoons dry sherry
1 tablespoon white vinegar
1 cup vegetable oil
1/2 cup lemon juice
1/2 cup Worcestershire sauce
1/4 cup prepared mustard

1 tablespoon sugar
1/4 teaspoon ginger
2 garlic cloves, chopped
1 tablespoon cracked pepper
3 chicken breasts
6 slices bacon, cut into 2-inch pieces

Combine the soy sauce, sherry, vinegar, vegetable oil, lemon juice, Worcestershire sauce and mustard in a bowl and mix well. Stir in the sugar, ginger, garlic and pepper.

Cut the chicken into bite-size pieces. Wrap with the bacon and secure with wooden picks. Add to the soy sauce mixture and marinate in the refrigerator for 1 hour.

Preheat the oven to 375 degrees. Arrange the chicken bites on a baking sheet and bake for 10 to 15 minutes or until the bacon is crisp and the chicken is cooked through.

Makes 24 to 30

First Fundraisers

Founded in 1935, the Junior League of Waco (then called the Service League) began holding fundraisers for the community—small ones by today's standards, but just as heart-felt. In its first year, the League held a Bridge Party that raised $93.50, a Men's Smoker that raised $107.02, a Fashion Tea that raised $106.30, and a Rummage Sale that raised $70.00.

Crab Crisps

1/2 cup (1 stick) margarine, softened
1 (6-ounce) jar Old English sharp
  Cheddar cheese spread

2 (6-ounce) cans crab meat
6 English muffins

Preheat the oven to 400 degrees. Beat the margarine in a mixing bowl until light and fluffy. Add the cheese spread and crab meat and mix well. Spread on the English muffins.

Cut the muffins into quarters and place on a baking sheet. Bake for 20 minutes or until the edges of the muffins are slightly crisp and the crab mixture is bubbly. You can freeze them to bake at a later date if preferred.

Makes 24

Crab Fondue

2 tablespoons butter
2 tablespoons all-purpose flour
1 cup chicken broth
8 ounces cream cheese, chopped
4 ounces Velveeta cheese, chopped
1/4 cup sherry

1 tablespoon minced onion
2 or 3 drops of Tabasco sauce
4 ounces canned or fresh crab meat or
  crawfish tails, drained
chopped fresh parsley
cubed French bread

Melt the butter in a saucepan. Stir in the flour and cook until smooth, stirring constantly. Add the chicken broth and cook until thickened, stirring constantly. Stir in the cream cheese, Velveeta cheese, sherry, onion, Tabasco sauce and crab meat gradually, cooking over low to medium heat until the cheese is melted.

Spoon into a fondue pot and garnish with parsley. Serve with cubed bread for dipping.

Serves 6

Olive and Cheese Crostini

1/2 cup (1 stick) margarine or butter, softened
1/4 cup mayonnaise
2 cups (8 ounces) shredded mozzarella cheese
1/2 cup finely chopped black olives
2 tablespoons chopped parsley
1 teaspoon garlic powder
1 teaspoon onion powder
2 (16-ounce) French baguettes

Garnish: *chopped tomatoes and fresh basil*

Preheat the oven to 350 degrees. Combine the margarine, mayonnaise, mozzarella cheese, black olives, parsley, garlic powder and onion powder in a mixing bowl and mix until smooth.

Cut the baguettes into 1/2-inch slices. Spread the slices with the olive mixture. Place on a baking sheet and bake for 10 to 15 minutes or until bubbly. Garnish with tomatoes and basil.

Makes 30

Waco Children's Symphony

Since the 1930s, the Junior League has been an integral part in the life of the Waco Symphony, forming the Waco Symphony Society and co-sponsoring the Children's Symphony, where thousands of fourth and fifth graders were introduced to symphonic music. After the project was fully developed, the Junior League turned the Children's Symphony over to the Waco Symphony Council, and it is now supported by Baylor University. The admission charge to the symphony is 50 cents for each student, and the proceeds are used to fund Baylor music scholarships.

Crostini with Grilled Shrimp and Goat Cheese

2 pounds large shrimp, peeled and deveined
1/4 cup olive oil
3 tablespoons chopped fresh rosemary
2 garlic cloves, minced
cracked pepper to taste
1 sourdough baguette
olive oil
kosher salt to taste
4 ounces goat cheese with herbs
2 red bell peppers, roasted and chopped
4 ounces crimini mushrooms, chopped
chopped fresh rosemary to taste

Combine the shrimp with 1/4 cup olive oil, the rosemary, garlic and pepper in a sealable plastic bag. Marinate in the refrigerator for 30 minutes or longer. Remove the shrimp from the marinade and grill over medium-hot coals for 3 to 5 minutes or until shrimp turn pink; do not overcook.

Preheat the oven to 375 degrees. Cut the baguette diagonally into eighteen 1/2-inch slices. Arrange on a baking sheet; brush with olive oil and sprinkle lightly with salt. Bake for 5 minutes or just until golden brown.

Spread the toasted slices evenly with the goat cheese. Top with the red bell peppers and mushrooms and bake until the cheese is heated through. Place the shrimp on the crostini and sprinkle with rosemary.

Makes 18

Stuffed Jalapeño Chiles

25 jalapeño chiles
1 (8-ounce) package cream cheese
25 slices bacon

Preheat the oven to 350 degrees. Wear gloves to slice the jalapeño chiles into halves lengthwise; discard the ribs and seeds. Cut the cream cheese into 50 small cubes. Place 1 cube of cream cheese in each chile half.

Cut the bacon slices into halves and wrap 1 piece of bacon around each chile, placing the seam underneath the chile. Place seam side down on a baking sheet with a low edge.

Bake the chiles for 1 hour or until the bacon is crisp. Serve warm or at room temperature. You can use Neufchâtel cheese and lean center-cut bacon to reduce the fat in this recipe, if desired.

Makes 50

Women in Wartime

All fundraising activities of the Junior League were tabled from 1941 to 1943 as a result of World War II. The organization's welfare activities continued with bureaus associated with the war effort. The League gave a series of Sunday afternoon parties for Air Force cadets.

Stuffed Mushrooms

24 *large fresh mushrooms*
1/4 cup (1/2 stick) butter, melted
8 ounces bulk pork sausage, crumbled
1 onion, finely chopped
1/4 cup dry sherry
1/2 cup fine white bread crumbs
3 tablespoons chopped fresh parsley
1/2 teaspoon thyme
1/4 teaspoon salt
1/8 teaspoon freshly ground pepper
2 tablespoons (about) heavy cream

Preheat the oven to 375 degrees. Remove and chop the mushroom stems. Brush the caps with some of the butter and place stem side up in a buttered 9×13-inch baking dish.

Brown the sausage with the onion in a skillet over low heat, stirring until crumbly; drain. Add the sherry and simmer until the liquid evaporates. Stir in the bread crumbs, parsley, thyme, salt and pepper.

Add the mushroom stems and enough cream to moisten the mixture to a consistency that will hold its shape in a spoon. Spoon into the mushroom caps and drizzle with the remaining butter. Bake for 20 minutes. Serve as an appetizer or side dish.

Serves 12

Mini Mexican Shells

1 (40-count) package won ton wrappers
vegetable oil
1 pound ground beef
1 envelope taco seasoning mix
1 envelope ranch salad dressing mix
1 cup mayonnaise
1 cup milk
1¹/₂ cups (6 ounces) shredded Monterey Jack cheese
1¹/₂ cups (6 ounces) shredded Cheddar cheese

Garnish: sour cream and chopped green onions

Preheat the oven to 350 degrees. Press each won ton wrapper into a miniature muffin cup and brush with vegetable oil. Bake for 5 minutes. Brown the ground beef in a skillet, stirring until crumbly; drain. Add the taco seasoning mix and cook using the package directions. Prepare the ranch salad dressing mix with the mayonnaise and milk using the package directions. Combine the ground beef mixture with 1¹/₂ cups of the salad dressing in a bowl. Add the Monterey Jack cheese and Cheddar cheese and mix well.

Spoon into the baked shells. Bake for 5 minutes or until the cheese melts. Garnish with a dollop of sour cream and chopped green onions and serve hot.

You can prepare the shells up to 2 days in advance and store in an airtight container. You can prepare the filling 1 day in advance and store in the refrigerator.

Makes 40

Bean and Cheese Dip

1 (15-ounce) can vegetarian refried beans
1/4 cup picante sauce
1 cup sour cream
2 ounces cream cheese, softened
1 envelope onion soup mix
10 drops of Tabasco sauce
1/4 cup (1 ounce) shredded Cheddar cheese
1/4 cup (1 ounce) shredded Monterey Jack cheese

Preheat the oven to 350 degrees. Combine the refried beans with the picante sauce, sour cream, cream cheese, onion soup mix and Tabasco sauce in a bowl and mix well.

Spoon into a baking dish and top with the Cheddar cheese and Monterey Jack cheese. Bake for 20 minutes. Serve hot with tortilla chips.

Serves 6

Corn Dip

1 (15-ounce) can Mexican-style corn, drained
1 jalapeño chile, chopped
1 (4-ounce) can chopped green chiles
1/4 cup chopped green onion
chopped cilantro (optional)
1/2 cup mayonnaise
1/2 cup sour cream
2 cups (8 ounces) shredded sharp Cheddar cheese

Combine the corn, jalapeño chile, green chiles, green onion, cilantro, mayonnaise, sour cream and Cheddar cheese in a medium bowl and mix well. Chill until serving time. Serve with corn chips or crackers.

Serves 8

Cowboy Caviar

2 (15-ounce) cans black-eyed peas, drained
1 (15-ounce) can field peas, drained
2 tablespoons chopped jalapeño chiles
1 (2-ounce) can sliced black olives, drained
1 (10-ounce) can tomatoes with green chiles, drained
3 or 4 small avocados, chopped
1/2 red onion, chopped
1 (8-ounce) bottle of Italian salad dressing
1/2 cup picante sauce

Combine the black-eyed peas, field peas, jalapeño chiles, black olives, tomatoes with green chiles, avocados and onion in a bowl. Add the salad dressing and picante sauce and mix well. Chill in the refrigerator for 8 hours or longer. Serve with tortilla chips.

Serves 12

Curry Chutney Dip

16 ounces cream cheese, softened
3 tablespoons curry powder
1 (5-ounce) jar chutney
2 bunches scallions, chopped
10 slices bacon, crisp-fried and crumbled
slivered almonds

Combine the cream cheese with the curry powder in a bowl and mix until smooth. Spread in a serving dish. Spoon the chutney over the top and sprinkle with the scallions, bacon and almonds. Serve with melba toast.

Serves 12

Pumpkin Tureen

1 (4-pound) pumpkin
2 tablespoons vegetable oil
4 garlic cloves, crushed
4 slices white bread, toasted
  and crumbled
1¹/2 cups (6 ounces) shredded
  Swiss cheese

¹/2 cup (2 ounces) shredded
  mozzarella cheese
2 cups half-and-half
¹/2 teaspoon freshly ground nutmeg
1 teaspoon salt
¹/2 teaspoon pepper

Preheat the oven to 350 degrees. Rinse and dry the pumpkin. Cut a 2-inch slice from the top and reserve; discard the seeds and fibers. Mix the vegetable oil and garlic in a small bowl and rub over the inside of the pumpkin. Place in a large roasting pan.

Alternate layers of toast crumbs, Swiss cheese and mozzarella cheese in the pumpkin until all are used. Combine the half-and-half, nutmeg, salt and pepper in a bowl and mix well. Pour over the layers in the pumpkin.

Replace the pumpkin top slice and bake for 2 hours, stirring the filling gently after 1¹/2 hours. Serve with buttered and toasted French bread fingers or crackers for dipping. You may double the filling recipe for a larger pumpkin.

Serves 8

Shop 'Til You Drop

In 1952, the Junior League established The Clothes Horse to provide quality second-hand clothing, supplied by their own donations, at affordable prices to people in need. In 1953, it was renamed The Thrift Shop and moved to its 4th Street location. In 1978, it was again renamed—The Penny Pincher—and its final location was at the Fairgate shopping center, where it provided a valuable community service until 2003.

Picadillo

2 pounds ground beef
1 cup chopped onion
2 tablespoons chopped garlic
1 cup chopped bell pepper
1 (15-ounce) can stewed tomatoes,
    chopped
2 cups peeled and chopped potatoes
1 or 2 (4-ounce) cans sliced mushrooms,
    drained
1 (4-ounce) can chopped pimento
1 (4-ounce) can chopped green chiles
chopped jalapeño chiles to taste

1 (4-ounce) can chopped black olives,
    drained
1 cup raisins
1 cup slivered almonds
$1/4$ cup Worcestershire sauce
2 (10-ounce) cans beef broth
2 (6-ounce) cans tomato paste
$1/2$ teaspoon cumin
$1/2$ teaspoon oregano
$2^1/2$ teaspoons salt
$1/4$ teaspoon cayenne pepper
$1/4$ teaspoon black pepper

Brown the ground beef with the onion and garlic in a Dutch oven, stirring until crumbly; drain. Add the bell pepper, tomatoes, potatoes, mushrooms, pimento, green chiles, jalapeño chiles, olives, raisins and almonds and mix well.

Stir in the Worcestershire sauce, beef broth, tomato paste, cumin, oregano, salt, cayenne pepper and black pepper. Simmer over low to medium heat for 1 to 2 hours or longer. Spoon into a serving bowl and serve with chips. You can also serve this as a taco filling or as a main dish.

Serves 30

Queso Flameado

1 large onion, slivered
1 large poblano chile, slivered
2 garlic cloves, chopped
2 or 3 tablespoons olive oil
1 (7-ounce) jar salsa
1 (7-ounce) can champiñóns en escabèche
    (pickled mushrooms with jalapeño chiles and onions), drained
12 ounces Queso Asadero Mexican cheese, thickly sliced

Preheat the oven to 300 degrees. Sauté the onion, poblano chile and garlic in the olive oil in a saucepan until tender. Add the salsa and champiñóns and mix well.

Place the cheese in a 9- or 10-inch ovenproof baking dish. Bake for 15 to 20 minutes or just until melted; do not overcook. Spoon the onion mixture over the cheese and serve immediately with tortilla chips.

You can also spoon the mixture onto corn or flour tortillas and roll to enclose.

Serves 10

When Disaster Strikes

On May 11, 1953, one of the deadliest tornadoes in history struck downtown Waco, killing 111 people and leaving a massive path of destruction and a town devastated by loss. The Junior League sprang into action, using the training of its members to serve the community. The League also set up a fund to alleviate the strain placed on the social services agencies that were affected by the tornado.

Black Bean and Corn Salsa

1 (16-ounce) can black beans, drained
1 (16-ounce) can whole kernel corn, drained
1 (4-ounce) can chopped jalapeño chiles
1 (4-ounce) can chopped green chiles
1/4 cup chopped onion
12 cherry tomatoes, chopped
4 to 5 tablespoons chopped cilantro, or to taste
juice of 1 small lime
salt and pepper to taste

Mix the black beans and corn in a bowl. Add the jalapeño chiles, green chiles, onion, tomatoes, cilantro, lime juice, salt and pepper and mix well. Chill in the refrigerator for 1 to 2 hours.

Serves 12

South of the Border Salsa

2 (16-ounce) cans stewed tomatoes
2 jalapeño chiles, chopped
1/2 cup chopped green onions
1/4 cup chopped cilantro
1/4 cup lime juice
2 tablespoons garlic powder
2 tablespoons cumin
salt and pepper to taste

Combine the tomatoes, jalapeño chiles, green onions and cilantro in a blender. Add the lime juice, garlic powder, cumin, salt and pepper. Process until smooth. Spoon into a serving bowl and serve with chips or tortillas.

Serves 16

Pico de Gallo

2 large tomatoes, chopped
1/2 onion, finely minced
2 jalapeño chiles, seeded and chopped

1/2 bunch cilantro, minced
juice of 1 lemon
1/2 to 1 teaspoon salt

Combine the tomatoes, onion, jalapeño chiles and cilantro in a bowl. Add the lemon juice and sprinkle with salt; mix gently. Chill for 4 hours or longer, stirring twice.

Serves 8

Salsa Verde

3 green tomatoes, chopped
4 small tomatillos, chopped
2 to 4 jalapeño chiles, chopped
6 to 8 garlic cloves
1 teaspoon salt

2 tablespoons olive oil
beer or water
3 avocados, coarsely chopped
1 bunch cilantro, chopped with stems
2 cups sour cream

Combine the tomatoes, tomatillos, jalapeño chiles, garlic, salt and olive oil in a saucepan. Cover and bring to a boil. Reduce the heat to a simmer and simmer for 20 to 25 minutes, stirring and adding beer or water as needed to prevent drying out. Cool to room temperature.

Process 1/3 of the mixture at a time with 1/3 of the avocados and cilantro in a blender until smooth. Combine the batches in a large bowl and stir in the sour cream. Chill in the refrigerator for 4 hours or longer to improve the flavor. You can freeze leftovers, if desired.

Serves 8 to 10

Heart of Texas Shrimp Dip

16 ounces cream cheese
1/2 cup mayonnaise
6 tablespoons dry white wine
1 garlic clove, minced
2 teaspoons grated onion
2 teaspoons prepared mustard
2 teaspoons sugar
1/2 teaspoon seasoned salt
1 pound fresh shrimp, cooked, peeled,
    deveined and chopped

Melt the cream cheese in a medium saucepan over low heat. Stir in the mayonnaise, wine, garlic, onion, mustard, sugar, and seasoned salt. Add the shrimp and cook until heated through. Spoon into a chafing dish and serve warm with crackers.

Serves 8 to 10

Shrimp and Salsa

4 ounces medium shrimp, cooked
3/4 to 1 cup salsa
2 teaspoons chopped fresh cilantro
1 (8-ounce) package cream cheese, softened
2 green onions, chopped

Peel, devein and chop the shrimp. Combine the salsa and cilantro in a bowl and mix well. Place the cream cheese on a serving plate and spoon the salsa mixture over the top. Top with the shrimp and sprinkle with the green onions. Serve with tortilla chips.

Serves 6 to 8

Dilly Artichoke Cheese Spread

1 (6-ounce) jar marinated artichoke
    hearts, drained
1 cup (4 ounces) grated Parmesan cheese
8 ounces cream cheese, softened
$^1/_2$ cup mayonnaise
$^1/_2$ teaspoon dill weed
2 garlic cloves, crushed

Preheat the oven to 375 degrees. Chop the artichoke hearts. Combine the chopped artichoke hearts, Parmesan cheese, cream cheese, mayonnaise, dill weed and garlic in a bowl and mix well. Spoon into a baking dish and bake for 15 minutes. Serve hot with crackers.

Serves 6 to 8

Dried Beef Cheese Balls

3 ounces dried beef, chopped
$^3/_4$ cup chopped green onions
1 (4-ounce) can chopped black olives
24 ounces cream cheese, softened
chopped pecans, crushed black peppercorns,
    red pepper flakes, poppy seeds and/or
    chopped fennel greens

Combine the dried beef with the green onions, black olives and cream cheese in a bowl and mix well. Shape into small balls. Roll in chopped pecans, black peppercorns, red pepper flakes and/or chopped fennel greens.
You may also shape the mixture into a large ball and roll in pecans or mix the pecans into the cheese ball. Serve with crackers.

Serves 12

Better Cheddar Spread

4 cups (16 ounces) shredded sharp
 Cheddar cheese
1 onion, grated
1 garlic clove, crushed
1/2 cup chopped parsley
3/4 cup mayonnaise
1/2 teaspoon Tabasco sauce
1 cup chopped pecans
1 cup strawberry preserves

Combine the Cheddar cheese, onion, garlic, parsley, mayonnaise and Tabasco sauce in a bowl and mix well. Oil a 3-cup ring mold and sprinkle half the pecans in the mold. Pack the cheese mixture into the mold.

Chill the mold in the refrigerator. Invert onto a serving plate and fill the center with the preserves. Sprinkle with the remaining 1/2 cup pecans. Serve with crackers.

Serves 20

Cheesy Pecan Spread

1 1/2 cups chopped green onions
2 cups chopped toasted pecans
3 cups (12 ounces) shredded Cheddar cheese
1 cup (about) mayonnaise
red or green jalapeño chile jelly

Combine the green onions, pecans and Cheddar cheese in a bowl and mix well. Add enough mayonnaise to bind the mixture. Press into a serving dish. Chill until serving time. Spread with jelly and serve with crackers.

Serves 10 to 12

Celebration Cheddar Cheesecake

1/4 cup fine bread crumbs
1/4 cup (1 ounce) shredded
   Cheddar cheese
24 ounces cream cheese, softened
4 green onions, chopped
2 small jalapeño chiles, minced

3 eggs
2 1/2 cups (10 ounces) shredded
   Cheddar cheese
1 cup sour cream
2 tablespoons milk
8 ounces cooked ham, chopped

Preheat the oven to 325 degrees. Mix the bread crumbs and 1/4 cup Cheddar cheese in a bowl. Press over the bottom of a buttered 9-inch springform pan.

Beat the cream cheese in a mixing bowl until smooth. Add the green onions, jalapeño chiles, eggs, 2 1/2 cups Cheddar cheese, sour cream, milk and half the ham; mix well. Pour half the mixture into the prepared crust. Sprinkle with the remaining ham and pour the remaining filling carefully over the ham.

Bake for 1 hour or until the center is set. Let stand for 30 minutes. Place on a serving plate. Loosen the edge of the cheesecake from the side of the pan with a knife and remove the side of the pan. Serve at room temperature with corn chips or crackers. Store in the refrigerator.

Serves 16

Historic Waco Foundation

In 1956, the Junior League helped purchase and restore the Fort House, one of the city's oldest historic homes. The League was instrumental in restoring the house, which later became a museum and part of Historic Waco Foundation. The League and its members continued to support Historic Waco Foundation by volunteering for the Brazos River Festival and Christmas on the Brazos, and by serving as docents for its five historic home museums.

Fiesta Spread

2¹/₂ to 3 cups (10 to 12 ounces)
  shredded Cheddar cheese
8 ounces cream cheese, softened
1 tablespoon chopped garlic
1 tablespoon chicken bouillon granules,
  or 1 crushed chicken bouillon cube
2 tablespoons lemon juice

10 to 12 drops of Tabasco sauce, or
  to taste
1 onion, chopped
1 tomato, chopped
1 (4-ounce) can chopped green chiles
1/2 cup chopped cilantro (optional)
1 cup coarsely chopped pecans (optional)

Combine the Cheddar cheese, cream cheese, garlic, bouillon, lemon juice and Tabasco sauce in a food processor or mixing bowl. Process or mix until smooth. Stir in the onion, tomato, green chiles, cilantro and pecans by hand.

Chill in the refrigerator for 2 hours or up to 5 days. Spoon into a serving dish and serve with crackers or melba rounds. To store for a longer time, you can substitute onion flakes, granulated garlic and sun-dried tomatoes for the fresh onions, garlic and tomatoes.

Serves 6 to 8

Having A Ball

"Carnival in Venice" was the theme of the first Charity Ball, held on February 6, 1960. Seven hundred fifty people attended the ball, which netted $5,124.59. Tickets were $20 per couple and included coffee, sweet rolls, and set-ups. Memorable Charity Ball themes throughout the years included "A Space Odyssey," "S.S. Eighty Lady," and "Puttin' on the Ritz." In 2004 and 2005, Charity Ball was voted "Best Fundraiser" by Wacoan *magazine. In its most profitable year, the Ball raised more than $200,000 for Junior League projects and community grants.*

Almond Tea

2 cups water
3 tea bags
1 cup sugar
1 teaspoon vanilla extract

juice of 3 lemons, or 6 tablespoons
    bottled lemon juice
1 1/2 teaspoons almond extract
6 cups water

Bring 2 cups water to a boil in a saucepan. Reduce the heat to a simmer and add the tea bags. Simmer for 5 minutes. Add the sugar, vanilla, lemon juice and almond extract. Simmer until the sugar dissolves, stirring occasionally.

Discard the tea bags and combine with 6 cups water in a pitcher. Chill until serving time. Serve over ice.

Makes 2 quarts

Fruity Mint Tea

6 cups water
5 individual tea bags or
    2 large tea bags
6 large mint sprigs
1 1/2 to 2 cups sugar
2 cups pineapple juice

3/4 cup fresh lemon juice,
    3 to 4 large lemons
2 cups ginger ale

Garnish: *fresh mint sprigs*

Bring the water to a boil in a saucepan. Remove from the heat and add the tea bags and mint; let stand for 5 to 10 minutes. Discard the tea bags and mint. Pour into a refrigerator container.

Add the sugar, pineapple juice and lemon juice and mix well. Chill until serving time or for up to several days. Add the ginger ale at serving time. Serve over ice and garnish with fresh mint.

Serves 12

Breakfast Slush

1 (12-ounce) can frozen orange juice concentrate, thawed
1 (6-ounce) can frozen lemonade concentrate, thawed
1 (15-ounce) can fruit cocktail
1 (8-ounce) can crushed pineapple
2 or 3 bananas, chopped or sliced
ginger ale or lemon-lime soda

Combine the orange juice concentrate, lemonade concentrate, undrained fruit cocktail, pineapple and bananas in a freezer-safe container; mix well. Cover and freeze for 8 hours or longer. Scoop the frozen mixture into small glasses and add a splash of ginger ale to serve.

Serves 8 to 10

Strawberry-Banana Punch

2 (12-ounce) cans frozen lemonade concentrate, thawed
2 (12-ounce) cans frozen orange juice concentrate, thawed
1 quart (4 cups) unsweetened pineapple juice
1 banana, mashed
1 (10-ounce) package frozen sliced strawberries, thawed
4 (12-ounce) cans water
1 quart (4 cups) sparkling water

Combine the lemonade concentrate, orange juice concentrate, pineapple juice, banana, strawberries and water in a large container pitcher and mix well. Chill until serving time. Combine with the sparkling water in a punch bowl at serving time and mix gently.

Serves 24

Heart-Stopper Punch

1 quart (4 cups) brewed coffee, cooled
1 cup sugar
1 tablespoon vanilla extract
1/4 teaspoon orange extract (optional)
1/2 teaspoon cinnamon
1/4 teaspoon ground cloves (optional)
1 gallon milk
1 quart chocolate ice cream, softened

Combine the coffee, sugar, vanilla and orange extract, cinnamon and cloves in a large bowl and stir to mix well and dissolve the sugar. Stir in the milk and chill until serving time.

Place the ice cream in a punch bowl and break up with a spoon. Pour the coffee mixture over the ice cream and mix well. You can add Kahlúa, if desired.

Serves 30

Freezer Milk Punch

1/2 cup water
1 cup sugar
1 fifth of bourbon
3 quarts (12 cups) milk
1 tablespoon vanilla extract
1/2 gallon vanilla ice cream, softened
nutmeg to taste

Bring the water and sugar to a boil in a saucepan, stirring to dissolve the sugar. Cool to room temperature. Combine the bourbon, milk and vanilla in a freezer-safe container and mix well. Add the sugar water and mix well. Freeze for 8 hours or longer.

Remove from the freezer 1 hour before serving. Place in a large punch bowl and add the ice cream, mixing with a wooden spoon. Sprinkle with nutmeg.

Serves 24

Champagne Punch

4 cups sugar
3 quarts (12 cups) ice water
juice of 12 lemons
1 (20-ounce) can crushed pineapple
1 quart (4 cups) sweet sauterne
1 quart fresh strawberries, sliced
2 bottles of champagne

Garnish: *ring mold made with the
punch mixture, strawberries and
mint sprigs*

Dissolve the sugar in the water in a large container. Add the lemon juice, pineapple and sauterne and mix well. Chill in the refrigerator until serving time. Combine with the strawberries and champagne in a punch bowl at serving time and mix gently.

To decorate with an ice ring, freeze a portion of the punch mixture in a ring mold. Add strawberries and mint sprigs and fill with the punch mixture. Freeze until serving time and float in the punch.

Serves 30

Sangria

2 bottles of red wine
1 cup brandy
6 tablespoons Cointreau
1 (2-liter) bottle of lemon-lime soda
1 cup sugar

juice of 2 oranges
juice of 1 lemon
juice of 2 limes

Garnish: *1 lemon, sliced*

Combine the wine, brandy, Cointreau, lemon-lime soda, sugar, orange juice, lemon juice and lime juice in a pitcher and mix well to dissolve the sugar. Garnish with lemon slices and serve over ice.

Serves 16

Heart-Warming Wassail

2 cups orange juice
2 cups cranberry juice
8 cups apple juice
3/4 cup sugar
1 teaspoon whole cloves
1 teaspoon whole allspice
2 cinnamon sticks

Combine the orange juice, cranberry juice, apple juice and sugar in a 12-cup percolator. Place the cloves, allspice and cinnamon sticks in the basket of the percolator. Run the percolator through its cycle and serve.

To make on the stovetop, tie the spices in a cheesecloth and combine with the juices and sugar in a saucepan. Simmer for 10 minutes. You can add rum, if desired.

Makes 12 cups

Chocolate Martini

1 1/2 ounces (3 tablespoons) vodka
2 ounces (1/4 cup) Godiva Chocolate Cream liqueur
1 ounce (2 tablespoons) Kahlúa
4 to 6 ice cubes
chocolate syrup

Combine the vodka, Godiva Chocolate Cream liqueur, Kahlúa and ice cubes in a shaker and shake to mix well. Add enough chocolate syrup to a martini glass to coat the inside and swirl to coat evenly. Pour the martini into the glass and serve immediately.

Serves 1

Toss in some…

Soups & Salads & Sandwiches

Tomato, potato, hearty cheese soup—

Enjoy them at home or share with a group.

Follow with a plate of luscious greens;

Add avocados and oranges to keep it lean.

This chapter graciously underwritten by Providence Healthcare Network

Tomato Basil Soup

1 (14-ounce) can tomato sauce
1 (10-ounce) can tomato soup
2 (14-ounce) cans chicken broth
2 (14-ounce) cans diced tomatoes
14 to 20 fresh basil leaves
1/4 cup (1/2 stick) butter

1 to 2 cups half-and-half or fat-free
   half-and-half
Cheese Petits Fours (below)

Garnish: grated Parmesan cheese

Combine the tomato sauce, tomato soup and chicken broth in a saucepan and mix well. Simmer for 30 minutes. Purée the tomatoes and basil in a food processor. Add to the soup and simmer for 15 to 20 minutes.

Stir in the butter and half-and-half. Cook until the butter melts. Serve with Cheese Petits Fours and garnish with Parmesan cheese.

Serves 10

Cheese Petits Fours

1 cup (2 sticks) butter, softened
2 (4-ounce) jars Old English cheese spread
garlic, basil and/or red pepper to taste (optional)
1 loaf thinly sliced white bread

Preheat the oven to 350 degrees. Cream the butter, cheese spread, garlic, basil and red pepper in a mixing bowl until smooth. Trim the crusts from the bread and spread with some of the cheese mixture. Arrange into stacks of 3 slices and cut each stack into quarters.

Spread the tops and sides of the quarters lightly with the remaining cheese mixture and place on a baking sheet. Bake for 12 to 15 minutes or until golden brown. You can serve these with soup or as an appetizer.

Makes 2 to 3 dozen

Shrimp Gumbo

8 slices bacon
12 ounces okra, chopped
1 onion, chopped
2 garlic cloves, chopped
2 celery ribs, chopped
1 (29-ounce) can diced tomatoes

1 bay leaf
2^1/$_2$ pounds shrimp, peeled and deveined
^{1}/$_2$ teaspoon salt
^{1}/$_4$ teaspoon pepper
hot cooked rice

Cook the bacon in a cast-iron skillet or a sauté pan until crisp; remove to paper towels to drain and reserve the drippings in the skillet. Break the bacon into bite-size pieces.

Add the okra to the drippings in the skillet and sear over medium heat. Add the onion, garlic and celery and sauté for 5 minutes. Combine the sautéed vegetables with the tomatoes and bay leaf in a 6-quart saucepan and mix well. Add the shrimp, bacon, salt and pepper.

Simmer for 30 minutes. Remove the bay leaf and serve the gumbo over rice. You can refrigerate for 8 hours or longer and reheat to improve the flavor.

Serves 6

Texas Chowder

1 pound bulk pork sausage
1 green bell pepper, chopped
1 red bell pepper, chopped
1 onion, chopped
2 (10-ounce) cans cream of potato soup
2 soup cans water

2 (16-ounce) cans cream-style corn
2 cups (8 ounces) shredded
   Cheddar cheese
2^1/$_2$ cups milk
1 tablespoon Worcestershire sauce
1 tablespoon chicken bouillon granules

Brown the sausage with the bell peppers and onion in a large saucepan, stirring until crumbly; drain. Add the soup, water, corn, Cheddar cheese, milk, Worcestershire sauce and chicken bouillon; mix well. Simmer until heated through.

Serves 6

Hearty Cheese Soup

1/4 cup (1/2 stick) butter
3 green onions, chopped
2 carrots, grated
3 celery ribs, finely chopped
1 (10-ounce) can chicken broth
3 (10-ounce) cans cream of potato soup

2 cups (8 ounces) shredded medium or
    sharp Cheddar cheese
1 cup sour cream
salt and pepper to taste
milk (optional)

Melt the butter in a 3-quart saucepan or Dutch oven. Add the green onions, carrots and celery and sauté until tender. Add the chicken broth and simmer, covered, for 20 minutes.

Stir in the soup, Cheddar cheese and sour cream. Cook over low heat until the cheese melts, stirring to mix well. Season with salt and pepper. Add milk if needed for the desired consistency.

Serves 6

Cheesy Chicken and Cabbage Soup

1 chicken
1 envelope Butter Buds
3 large Idaho potatoes, or 24 ounces
    frozen cubed or shredded potatoes
1 onion, grated or chopped
1 cup chopped celery

1 cup chopped carrots
1 head cabbage, sliced
4 chicken bouillon cubes
pepper to taste
12 ounces Velveeta cheese, chopped

Combine the chicken with enough water to cover in a saucepan. Cook until tender; drain, reserving the broth. Cut the chicken into small pieces, discarding the skin and bones.

Combine the chicken with the reserved chicken broth, Butter Buds, potatoes, onion, celery, carrots, cabbage, bouillon cubes and pepper in a saucepan and mix well.

Cook over medium heat for 1 1/2 hours. Add the cheese to the soup and let stand until the cheese melts. Stir to mix well and serve.

Serves 6

Beef and Vegetable Stew

3 pounds lean ground beef
1 or 2 onions, chopped
2 garlic cloves, minced
2 tablespoons butter
3 (10-ounce) cans beef broth
2 (10-ounce) cans tomatoes with
   green chiles
1 (15-ounce) can tomato sauce
1¹/₂ cups chopped unpeeled potatoes

1 cup chopped carrots
1 cup chopped celery
1 (14-ounce) can French-style
   green beans
1¹/₂ cups dry red wine
2 tablespoons parsley flakes
1 tablespoon chopped basil
salt and pepper to taste

Brown the ground beef in a large skillet, stirring until crumbly; drain. Sauté the onions and garlic in the butter in a large saucepan until tender. Add the ground beef and mix well.

Add the beef broth, tomatoes with green chiles, tomato sauce, potatoes, carrots, celery, green beans, wine, parsley flakes, basil, salt and pepper and mix well. Bring to a boil and reduce the heat. Simmer for 30 to 40 minutes or until the vegetables are tender.

Serves 8

Bookworms

A joint effort of the Junior League, the City of Waco, and the Cooper Foundation made possible the Lake Air Station of the Waco Public Library in 1967. It was located in the Lake Air Mall. In 1968, the station was renamed the R.B. Hoover Branch in memory of the Cooper Foundation's Executive Director, who supported the Waco library system and was dedicated to making books available to people in all areas of town.

Spicy Vegetable Garden Chowder

2 cups water
1¹/2 cups peeled and chopped potatoes
1 cup thinly sliced carrots
1 cup thinly sliced celery
¹/3 cup chopped onion
¹/2 teaspoon salt
1¹/2 teaspoons pepper
¹/2 cup (1 stick) butter or margarine
¹/4 cup all-purpose flour
1 cup milk, warmed
¹/2 cup chicken broth, warmed
2 cups (8 ounces) shredded Cheddar cheese
¹/4 teaspoon dill weed
12 to 16 ounces Polish sausage,
*   sliced ¹/4 inch thick and cooked*

Bring 2 cups water to a boil in a 2-quart saucepan and add the potatoes, carrots, celery, onion, salt and pepper. Simmer, covered, for 15 minutes or until the vegetables are tender.

Melt the butter in a 4-quart saucepan. Stir in the flour and cook until smooth. Remove from the heat and stir in the milk and chicken broth gradually. Bring to a boil and cook for 1 minute, stirring constantly. Add the cheese and stir to melt completely.

Add the vegetables with any remaining water, dill weed and sausage. Cook until heated through, adding ¹/2 to 1 cup additional water if needed for the desired consistency. Serve with a salad and corn bread.

Serves 4

Mexican Fiesta Salad with Cilantro Dressing

Salad
2/3 cup dried black beans, rinsed
    and picked
2 tablespoons olive oil
2 tablespoons white wine vinegar
1/2 teaspoon salt
1/2 cup chopped red onion
1 cup corn kernels
1/2 cup chopped green bell pepper
2 cups thinly sliced iceberg lettuce
11/2 cups seeded and chopped tomatoes
1 cup (4 ounces) shredded Monterey
    Jack cheese

1/2 avocado, cut into 6 slices
4 slices lean bacon, crisp-cooked
    and crumbled

Cilantro Dressing
3 to 5 jalapeño chiles, seeded
1/4 cup white wine vinegar
1 garlic clove
1 teaspoon salt
2/3 cup olive oil
1/2 cup packed fresh cilantro

Garnish: cilantro sprig

For the salad, combine the beans with enough water to cover by 2 inches in a large saucepan. Bring to a boil and boil for 3 minutes. Remove from the heat and let stand for 10 minutes. Drain the beans and add enough water to cover the beans by 2 inches. Bring to a boil and reduce the heat. Simmer for 45 minutes or just until tender; drain and rinse under cold water. Combine with the olive oil, vinegar and salt in a bowl and mix well. Chill, covered, for 2 to 24 hours. Drain the beans and add the onion, toss to mix well.

Toss the corn and bell pepper in a bowl. Place the lettuce in a 2-quart bowl. Reserve 2 tablespoons of the beans, 1 tablespoon of the tomatoes and 1 tablespoon of the corn mixture. Layer the remaining beans, tomatoes and corn mixture over the lettuce. Top with the cheese. Arrange the avocado slices in a spoke design over the salad and sprinkle the bacon and reserved beans, tomatoes and corn mixture between the avocado slices. Garnish with a cilantro sprig and serve with the dressing.

For the dressing, purée the jalapeño chiles with the vinegar, garlic and salt in a blender. Add the olive oil in a steady stream, processing constantly. Add the cilantro and process until finely chopped. Chill in the refrigerator.

Serves 4

Roasted Mushroom Salad

Balsamic Vinaigrette
5 tablespoons balsamic vinegar
1 tablespoon Dijon mustard
$^1/_2$ teaspoon crumbled dried thyme
$^2/_3$ cup olive oil
salt and pepper to taste

Salad
12 ounces fresh mushrooms,
    cut into halves or quarters
1 head red leaf lettuce, torn
1 head Bibb lettuce, torn
1 head curly endive, torn
$^1/_2$ small red onion, thinly sliced
$^1/_2$ bunch fresh chives, cut into 1-inch pieces
salt and pepper to taste

For the vinaigrette, combine the balsamic vinegar, Dijon mustard and thyme in a small bowl and whisk to mix well. Whisk in the olive oil gradually and season with salt and pepper.

For the salad, place the mushrooms on a baking sheet and pour $^1/_4$ cup of the vinaigrette over the top, tossing to coat evenly. Grill the mushrooms on a foil-covered grill or in a grill basket until golden brown but still moist. Cool to room temperature.

Combine the lettuces, endive, onion and chives in a large bowl. Add the remaining vinaigrette and season with salt and pepper; toss to coat well. Spoon onto salad plates and spoon the mushrooms over the top.

Serves 10

Crunchy Asian Slaw

Slaw Dressing
1 cup canola oil
1/2 cup white vinegar
1/2 cup sugar
seasonings from 2 packages beef-flavor
    ramen noodles

Slaw
2 (12-ounce) packages broccoli slaw mix
2 bunches green onions, chopped
1 cup sunflower seeds
1 cup toasted chopped pecans
noodles from 2 packages beef-flavor
    ramen noodles

For the dressing, combine the canola oil, vinegar, sugar and seasoning packets from the ramen noodles in a bowl and whisk to mix well. Chill until serving time.

For the slaw, combine the broccoli slaw mix, green onions, sunflower seeds and pecans in a large bowl and mix well. Crumble the ramen noodles over the salad and add the dressing just before serving; toss to coat well.

You can prepare all the ingredients for this salad a day in advance and store separately in the refrigerator to assemble at serving time.

Serves 8 to 10

Glazed Sugared Pecans

1 cup sugar
1/4 cup orange juice

1 teaspoon cinnamon
4 cups pecans

Bring the sugar, orange juice and cinnamon to a boil over medium heat. Add the pecans and cook until the pecans are glazed. Remove from the heat and stir to separate the pecans. Spread on waxed paper to cool and store in a sealable plastic bag.

Makes 4 cups

Seasonal Salads with Raspberry Poppy Seed Dressing

Raspberry Poppy Seed Dressing
2 cups mayonnaise
1/3 cup half-and-half
1/2 cup raspberry vinegar
3 tablespoons raspberry jam
2/3 cup sugar
2 tablespoons poppy seeds

Spring or Summer Salad
spinach
sliced fresh strawberries
toasted sliced almonds
hard-cooked eggs, sliced (optional)

Fall or Winter Salad
spinach
dried cranberries
chopped apples (optional)
crumbled feta cheese
Glazed Sugared Pecans (page 55)

For the dressing, combine the mayonnaise, half-and-half, raspberry vinegar, raspberry jam, sugar and poppy seeds in a blender and process until smooth. Store in a covered container in the refrigerator for up to 1 week.

For a spring or summer salad, combine spinach, sliced fresh strawberries and almonds with the dressing in a bowl and toss to coat well. Garnish with hard-cooked eggs, if desired.

For a fall or winter salad, combine spinach, dried cranberries, chopped apples, feta cheese and desired amount of Glazed Sugared Pecans with the dressing in a bowl and toss.

To carry the salad to a friend, place salad ingredients in separate clear bags and tie with raffia. Arrange in a basket, bowl or pretty bag and add a jar of dressing, some fresh homemade bread, some flowers from the garden and a special note.

Serves 8 to 10

Strawberry Salad with Poppy Seed Dressing

1 cup pecans
1 head red leaf lettuce, torn
2 cups strawberries
12 ounces bacon, crisp-cooked and crumbled
1/2 small red onion, thinly sliced, or to taste
Poppy Seed Dressing (below)

Sprinkle the pecans in a sauté pan and toast over medium heat until golden brown. Cool to room temperature.

Layer the lettuce, strawberries, bacon, pecans and onion in a salad bowl. Add the desired amount of Poppy Seed Dressing and toss to coat evenly.

Serves 6

Poppy Seed Dressing

6 tablespoons white vinegar
3/4 cup sugar
1/2 teaspoon dry mustard
1/2 tablespoon poppy seeds
salt to taste
1 cup extra-virgin olive oil

Combine the vinegar, sugar, dry mustard, poppy seeds and salt in a bowl. Whisk in the olive oil gradually until smooth. Store in the refrigerator until serving time.

Makes 1 1/2 cups

Spinach Salad with Pecan Vinaigrette

1 (6-ounce) package spinach
1 or 2 pears, peeled and sliced
$^1/_2$ to $^3/_4$ cup dried cranberries
$^1/_2$ to $^3/_4$ cup crumbled feta cheese
Pecan Vinaigrette (below)

Layer the spinach, pears, dried cranberries and feta cheese in a salad bowl. Add the desired amount of Pecan Vinaigrette and toss to coat evenly.

Serves 4

Pecan Vinaigrette

$^1/_4$ cup balsamic vinegar
1 garlic clove, minced
2 tablespoons sugar
salt and pepper to taste
$^3/_4$ cup extra-virgin olive oil
$^1/_2$ cup toasted chopped pecans

Combine the vinegar, garlic, sugar, salt and pepper in a bowl. Whisk in the olive oil until smooth. Stir in the pecans and store in the refrigerator until serving time.

Makes 1$^1/_2$ cups

Sunflower Spinach Salad

2 packages ramen noodles
1/2 cup (1 stick) butter
1 (12-ounce) package baby spinach
1/2 cup chopped green onion
1 cup broccoli florets (optional)

1 cup mandarin oranges
1/2 cup sunflower seeds
3/4 cup slivered almonds
6 ounces crumbled feta cheese (optional)
Sweet-and-Sour Vinaigrette (below)

Crush the unopened packages of ramen noodles. Open the packages and remove and discard the seasoning packets. Sauté the crushed noodles in the butter in a skillet until golden brown; cool and store in airtight container.

Combine the spinach, green onions, broccoli, oranges, sunflower seeds, almonds and feta cheese in a bowl and toss to mix. Add the toasted noodles and Sweet-and-Sour Vinaigrette at serving time and toss to coat evenly.

Serves 8 to 10

Sweet-and-Sour Vinaigrette

1/2 cup red wine vinegar
1 tablespoon soy sauce
3/4 cup canola oil
1/2 cup sugar

Combine the vinegar, soy sauce, canola oil and sugar in a covered jar and shake to mix well. Store in the refrigerator until serving time.

Makes 1 1/4 cups

Butter Lettuce Salad with Pomegranate Vinaigrette

Candied Walnuts
1/4 cup confectioners' sugar
salt to taste
1 cup walnut halves

Salad
1 or 2 heads butter lettuce or
    Bibb lettuce
2 or 3 pears, such as red, Anjou,
    Bartlett and/or Asian, chopped
1/2 cup currants
2 tablespoons pomegranate seeds
Pomegranate Vinaigrette (below)

For the walnuts, preheat the oven to 350 degrees. Mix the confectioners' sugar and salt in a medium bowl. Bring a small saucepan of water to a boil and add the walnuts. Blanch for 3 minutes and drain well. Add to the confectioners' sugar mixture immediately and toss to coat evenly.

Spread on a baking sheet and bake for 10 minutes or until golden brown; watch carefully to avoid burning. Cool to room temperature and break or cut into smaller pieces.

For the salad, chill the serving plates in the freezer. Arrange the lettuce leaves on the chilled plates. Sprinkle with the pears, currants, candied walnuts and pomegranate seeds. Drizzle with the desired amount of Pomegranate Vinaigrette.

Serves 6

Pomegranate Vinaigrette

1/2 cup pomegranate juice
1/2 cup champagne vinegar
1 tablespoon honey

salt and white pepper to taste
1/2 cup olive oil
1/2 cup canola oil

Combine the pomegranate juice, vinegar and honey in a bowl and mix well. Season with salt and white pepper. Mix the olive oil and canola oil in a small bowl and whisk into the vinaigrette gradually.

Makes 2 cups

Greek Salad with Grilled Sirloin

1 pound sirloin steak
8 cups torn romaine
1 large red onion, sliced
2 tomatoes, chopped
8 pepperoncini
1¹/₂ cups crumbled feta cheese
black olives, capers and/or
 artichoke hearts (optional)
sea salt and pepper to taste
Basil Vinaigrette (below)

Grill the steak over medium heat until done to taste. Cover and let stand for 10 minutes. Cut into thin slices.

Divide the lettuce between 4 plates. Layer the onion, tomatoes, pepperoncini, feta cheese, black olives, capers and artichoke hearts over the lettuce. Sprinkle with sea salt and pepper. Top with the steak slices and drizzle with the desired amount of Basil Vinaigrette.

Serves 4

Basil Vinaigrette

3 tablespoons red wine vinegar
2 tablespoons chopped fresh basil
1 teaspoon Dijon mustard
salt and pepper to taste
¹/₂ cup olive oil

Combine the vinegar, basil, Dijon mustard, salt and pepper in a bowl and mix well. Whisk in the olive oil gradually. Store, covered, in the refrigerator.

Makes ³/₄ cup

Chicken and Almond Salad

3 cups chopped cooked chicken
1¹/₂ cups chopped celery
3 tablespoons lemon juice
¹/₂ cup chopped red apple
¹/₂ cup pineapple chunks
1 cup toasted almonds
1 cup mayonnaise
¹/₄ cup half-and-half

1 teaspoon dry mustard
1¹/₂ teaspoons salt
¹/₈ teaspoon pepper
ruffled lettuce

Garnish: pineapple slice halves,
parsley sprigs and apple slices

Combine the chicken, celery and lemon juice in a bowl and mix well. Chill for 1 hour. Add the chopped apple, pineapple and almonds.

Combine the mayonnaise, half-and-half, dry mustard, salt and pepper in a bowl and mix well. Add to the chicken mixture and toss to mix well. Spoon into a salad bowl lined with ruffled lettuce. Garnish with pineapple slices, parsley and apple slices.

Serves 8 to 10

Getting Creative

In 1975, the Junior League initiated the renovation of the Cameron House for the home of The Art Center and continued to provide funds and scholarships for classes and for the promotion of Art Center programs. In the past, the Junior League has provided volunteer docents. Today, Art Center Waco continues to encourage the appreciation of diverse art forms through exhibits and classes open to the community.

Artichoke and Rice Salad

1 (5^1/$_2$-ounce) package chicken-flavor
    rice mix
1 (14-ounce) can artichoke hearts,
    chopped
4 green onions, chopped

^{1}/$_2$ green bell pepper, chopped
black olives (optional)
^{1}/$_2$ cup mayonnaise
^{1}/$_2$ teaspoon curry powder

Cook the rice using the package directions and omitting the butter. Cool to room temperature. Add the artichoke hearts, green onions, bell pepper, black olives, mayonnaise and curry powder; mix well. Chill until serving time.

Serves 8 to 10

Wild Rice and Tuna Salad

1 (7-ounce) package wild rice mix
^{1}/$_2$ cup sour cream
1 cup mayonnaise or mayonnaise-type
    salad dressing
2 tablespoons chopped green onions
^{1}/$_2$ cup chopped celery

1 (6-ounce) can water-pack
    white tuna, drained
1 cup cashews

Garnish: *lettuce, tomato*
    and avocado

Cook the wild rice using the package directions. Drain any remaining liquid and remove to a large bowl.

Mix the sour cream, mayonnaise, green onions and celery in a small bowl. Add to the rice and mix well. Add the tuna and cashews and toss lightly to mix. Garnish with lettuce, tomato and avocado. Serve at room temperature. You can also chill and serve later, adding the cashews and garnishing at serving time.

Serves 8

Frozen Cranberry Salad

12 ounces whipped topping
8 ounces cream cheese, softened
$^1/_2$ cup sugar
1 teaspoon almond extract
1 (16-ounce) can whole cranberry sauce
1 (8-ounce) can crushed pineapple, drained
1 cup chopped pecans

Combine the whipped topping, cream cheese, sugar and almond extract in a mixing bowl and beat until smooth. Add the cranberry sauce, pineapple and pecans and mix well. Spoon into a 9×11-inch dish and freeze until firm. Cut into squares to serve.

Serves 12

Grape Salad

8 ounces cream cheese, softened
1 cup sour cream
$^1/_2$ cup sugar
2 pounds seedless green grapes
2 pounds seedless red grapes
$^1/_2$ cup packed brown sugar
$^1/_4$ cup ground pecans (optional)

Combine the cream cheese, sour cream and sugar in a mixing bowl and beat until smooth. Add the grapes and mix gently, coating well. Spoon into a salad bowl.

Mix the brown sugar and pecans in a small bowl and sprinkle over the grapes. Chill until serving time.

Serves 8

Frozen Fruit Salad

1 teaspoon unflavored gelatin
2 tablespoons lemon juice
1 banana, chopped
lemon juice
3 ounces cream cheese, softened
1/4 cup mayonnaise
salt to taste
1/2 cup evaporated milk, frozen until ice crystals form
1/2 cup sugar
1 (20-ounce) can fruit cocktail, drained
1/2 cup chopped nuts (optional)
lettuce leaves

Sprinkle the gelatin over 2 tablespoons lemon juice in a double boiler and let stand to soften. Cook over hot water until the gelatin dissolves completely. Sprinkle the banana with a small amount of lemon juice in a small bowl.

Combine the cream cheese, mayonnaise and salt in a mixing bowl and beat until smooth. Stir in the gelatin mixture.

Whip the evaporated milk in a mixing bowl, adding the sugar gradually as peaks begin to form and continuing to whip until stiff peaks form. Fold in the cream cheese mixture, fruit cocktail, banana and nuts.

Spoon into 7×11-inch dish lined with waxed paper. Freeze for 4 hours or until firm. Invert onto a platter and cut into thick slices. Place on lettuce-lined serving plates and let stand at room temperature for several minutes before serving.

Serves 8

Chicken Salad Sandwich Supreme

2 cups chopped cooked chicken
3/4 cup chopped celery
1/4 cup toasted sliced almonds
2 tablespoons chopped green olives
2 tablespoons chopped black olives
1 tablespoon sweet pickle relish

1 tablespoon dill pickle relish
2 hard-cooked eggs, chopped
1/2 cup mayonnaise
1 teaspoon lemon juice
4 croissants, split horizontally

Combine the chicken, celery, almonds, green olives, black olives, pickle relishes and eggs in a large bowl. Add the mayonnaise and lemon juice and mix well. Spread on the croissants to serve.

Serves 4

Parsley and Bacon Sandwiches

1 bunch parsley, chopped
2 pounds bacon, crisp-cooked
    and crumbled
1/2 to 3/4 cup mayonnaise

8 ounces cream cheese, softened
1/2 cup (1 stick) butter, softened
1/2 teaspoon garlic powder
48 thin slices bread

Combine the parsley, bacon, mayonnaise and cream cheese in a bowl and mix well. Blend the butter and garlic powder in a small bowl. Spread half the bread slices with the parsley and bacon mixture and half with the butter mixture. Place 1 of each together to form the sandwiches. Trim the crusts from the sandwiches and cut each sandwich into thirds.

Serves 24

Tailgate Sandwiches

Sandwich Dressing
1/2 cup (1 stick) butter
1 tablespoon prepared mustard
1 to 1 1/2 tablespoons Worcestershire sauce
1 1/2 teaspoons poppy seeds
1 tablespoon chopped onion

Sandwiches
6 kaiser rolls
shaved Honeysuckle White® Turkey
shaved ham
sliced Swiss cheese
sliced American cheese
chopped black olives (optional)

For the dressing, melt the butter in a saucepan or microwave. Combine with the mustard, Worcestershire sauce, poppy seeds and onion in a bowl and mix well.

For the sandwiches, preheat the oven to 375 degrees. Split the kaiser rolls horizontally. Spread 1 to 1 1/2 tablespoons of the dressing over the cut sides of the rolls. Layer the turkey, ham and cheeses on the bottom halves of the rolls and sprinkle with black olives. Top with the remaining roll halves.

Wrap the sandwiches in foil and bake for 10 to 15 minutes. You can freeze the sandwiches, thaw in the refrigerator and bake at serving time.

Serves 6

Main Dishes

Serve the entrée piping hot.

Delicious beef tenderloin hits the spot.

Pork or chicken, game or fish—

Just the right sauce makes the perfect dish.

This chapter graciously underwritten by Greg May Honda

Rolled Brisket Pot Roast

1 (3-pound) boneless brisket, trimmed
salt, pepper and garlic powder to taste
soy sauce
$^1/_3$ cup bacon drippings
1 cup chopped slab bacon
2 onions, sliced and separated
    into rings
4 celery ribs, thickly sliced
6 to 8 (or more) large carrots,
    peeled and thickly sliced
$^1/_4$ cup red wine vinegar
$^1/_2$ teaspoon sage
$^1/_2$ teaspoon thyme
1 bay leaf
small white potatoes with skins

Sprinkle the top side of the brisket with salt, pepper and garlic powder. Roll tightly from the thicker end and tie with string. Brush the surface with soy sauce and rub into the brisket. Sprinkle generously with salt and pepper and lightly with garlic powder.

Heat the bacon drippings in a deep saucepan. Add the rolled brisket and brown lightly on all sides. Add the bacon, onions, celery and carrots. Pour the vinegar over the top and sprinkle with the sage and thyme, rubbing the herbs lightly into the roll. Place the bay leaf on top.

Reduce the heat to medium and cook, covered, for 1 hour. Turn the brisket and add potatoes. Drizzle with a small amount of soy sauce and cook for $1^1/_2$ hours longer. Discard the bay leaf before serving. You can reduce the heat to cook longer, if desired.

Serves 6 to 8

Carne Guisada

1 (3-pound) chuck roast
1 to 3 tablespoons all-purpose flour
1 teaspoon salt
pepper to taste
^{1}/$_2$ cup vegetable oil

1 large onion, chopped
1 (16-ounce) can kidney beans, drained
1 (16-ounce) can tomatoes
^{1}/$_3$ cup dry red wine
2 (4-ounce) cans chopped green chiles

Cut the roast into 4 or 5 large pieces. Coat with a mixture of the flour, salt and pepper. Brown the pieces on all sides in the heated vegetable oil in a large Dutch oven. Remove the beef to a bowl.

Add the onion to the drippings in the Dutch oven and sauté until tender. Return the beef to the pan and add the beans, tomatoes, wine and green chiles. Cover and bring to a simmer. Simmer for 4 to 5 hours or until the meat is fork tender and shreds easily.

Remove the beef and shred. Return to the gravy and serve with tortillas, shredded cheese, jalapeño chiles and Mexican rice.

Serves 8

Helping Hospitals

Waco's first self-sustaining mobile baby incubator was made possible in 1979 through a Junior League grant of $2,500. The piece of equipment allowed hospital personnel to move critically ill infants to and from surgery and neonatal facilities, which were not available in Waco at that time.

Southwest Pot Roast

1 (1½-pound) pot roast
1 envelope chili seasoning mix
1½ cups dried pinto beans
2 (10-ounce) cans tomatoes with
    green chiles
1 (10-ounce) can cream of
    mushroom soup

1 (4-ounce) can chopped green chiles
½ cup water

Garnish: shredded cheese, sour
    cream, chopped onions and/or
    shredded lettuce

Rub the roast with the chili seasoning mix and place in a slow cooker. Sprinkle the uncooked pinto beans around the roast.

Combine the tomatoes with green chiles, soup and green chiles in a bowl. Fill the soup can with the water and add to the bowl; mix well. Pour over the roast.

Cook on High for 7 to 8 hours, adding water if the mixture appears to need it. Remove the roast from the slow cooker and shred. Return the shredded beef to the slow cooker and mix well.

Serve in taco shell bowls, in flour tortillas or over Spanish rice. Garnish with cheese, sour cream, onions and/or shredded lettuce.

Serves 6

Kids Kastle

In the late 1970s, there weren't many options for local stay-at-home moms to have a safe place for their children to play while they did volunteer work. The Junior League partnered with First United Methodist Church and proposed that if the church could provide the building, the Junior League would supervise a preschool and mother's day out program—with one League member serving as the director. Today, Kids Kastle is a large, thriving program that offers a nurturing place for children from six months to five years of age to play and learn.

Beef Tenderloin

1 (4-pound) beef tenderloin, trimmed
olive oil
kosher salt or other coarse salt

coarsely ground pepper
Peppered Mushroom Sauce (below)

Place the tenderloin in a roasting pan and brush with olive oil. Sprinkle with kosher salt and pepper. Let stand until room temperature before roasting.

Preheat the oven to 450 degrees. Roast the tenderloin for exactly 15 minutes. Turn off the oven and let the tenderloin remain in the oven for exactly 45 minutes for medium rare; do not open the oven door. Serve with the Peppered Mushroom Sauce.

You can also roast the tenderloin for 15 minutes and remove to a heated grill. Grill for 20 to 30 minutes or to 140 degrees on an instant-read meat thermometer.

Serves 10

Peppered Mushroom Sauce

1 shallot, finely chopped
3 tablespoons butter
2 tablespoons cracked pepper
1 teaspoon all-purpose flour
1/4 cup water

1/2 cup beef stock
1 1/2 teaspoons tomato paste
1/2 teaspoon Worcestershire sauce
Tabasco sauce to taste
1 1/2 cups thinly sliced mushrooms

Sauté the shallot in the butter in a sauté pan for 1 to 2 minutes and add the cracked pepper. Stir in the flour and cook until smooth, stirring constantly. Add the water and cook until slightly thickened, stirring constantly.

Stir in the beef stock, tomato paste, Worcestershire sauce and Tabasco sauce. Add mushrooms and simmer until done to taste.

Makes 2 cups

Peppercorn Tenderloin

2 teaspoons ground pink peppercorns
2 teaspoons ground green peppercorns
2 teaspoons ground black peppercorns
2 teaspoons ginger

1 1/2 teaspoons cardamom
8 garlic cloves, minced
1/2 cup soy sauce
1 pound beef tenderloin

Combine the pink peppercorns, green peppercorns, black peppercorns, ginger, cardamom and garlic with 2 tablespoons of the soy sauce in a small bowl and mix well. Rub the mixture over the tenderloin.

Place the tenderloin in a large sealable plastic bag and add the remaining soy sauce. Marinate in the refrigerator for 8 hours or longer, turning occasionally.

Preheat the oven to 425 degrees. Remove the tenderloin from the bag. Reserve the marinade for basting the beef as it roasts. Place the beef on a greased rack in a roasting pan and insert a meat thermometer into the thickest portion. Roast for 45 minutes or to 140 degrees for rare or 160 degrees for medium.

Serves 2

Making Beautiful Music Together

With their magnificent performances, the Junior League "Sunshine Singers," in 1979, began bringing smiles to the faces of senior citizens and children alike. Today, the Musical Therapy singers—mostly sustaining members of the Junior League—continue to perform weekly at nursing homes, childcare facilities, and community events. From golden oldies to holiday classics, this group is as versatile as it is fun. According to one long-time singer, there's nothing quite like seeing an older man's face light up when he hears a familiar tune from his youth.

Mushroom Beef Wellington

1 (3- to 4-pound) beef tenderloin
8 ounces mushrooms, finely chopped
2 tablespoons red wine
2 tablespoons butter
8 ounces cream cheese with chives, softened
1/4 cup seasoned dry bread crumbs
1 tablespoon chopped fresh chives
1/4 teaspoon salt
1 package frozen puff pastry, thawed
1 egg
1 teaspoon cold water

Preheat the oven to 425 degrees. Roll the tenderloin and tie at 1-inch intervals. Place in a roasting pan and insert a meat thermometer. Roast for 45 to 50 minutes or to 135 degrees on the meat thermometer. Cool to room temperature.

Combine the mushrooms, wine and butter in a saucepan. Cook until the liquid evaporates. Add the cream cheese, bread crumbs, chives and salt and mix well.

Overlap the puff pastry sheets about 1/2 inch on a lightly floured surface to form a 12×14-inch rectangle. Cut to make a rectangle 2 1/2 inches larger than the tenderloin.

Place the tenderloin on a clean surface and remove the strings. Coat the top and sides with the mushroom mixture. Place the pastry over the tenderloin and tuck under the ends and edges. Brush with a mixture of the egg and water.

Place on a baking sheet and bake for 20 to 25 minutes longer or until the pastry is golden brown. Let stand for 10 minutes before slicing.

Serves 6 to 8

Steak Santa Fe

6 garlic cloves, minced
1 cup vegetable oil
4 beef fillets, rib eye steak or New York strip steaks
4 bunches green onions, chopped
2 (4-ounce) cans chopped green chiles
2 large tomatoes, chopped
1 pound fresh mushrooms, chopped
1/2 cup (1 stick) butter, melted
salt to taste
1 1/3 cups packed brown sugar

Mix the garlic and vegetable oil in a bowl. Rub into the steaks in a bowl. Cover and marinate in the refrigerator for 8 to 10 hours.

Sauté the green onions, undrained chiles, tomatoes and mushrooms in the melted butter in a sauté pan until tender.

Preheat a charcoal grill. Remove the steaks from the marinade. Sprinkle with salt and roll in brown sugar, patting so the brown sugar will adhere. Grill until done to taste. Serve with the sautéed vegetables.

Serves 4

Stuffed Sirloin Steak Rolls

8 ounces bulk pork sausage
1/2 cup bread crumbs
1 egg
1 1/2 tablespoons capers
2 garlic cloves, crushed
salt and pepper to taste
2 pounds boneless sirloin or round steak,
    sliced thin lengthwise
3 tablespoons vegetable oil
1/2 cup water
2 teaspoons marjoram
1 medium onion, sliced
wine (optional)

Brown the sausage in a skillet, stirring until crumbly; drain. Combine with the bread crumbs, egg, capers, garlic, salt and pepper in a small bowl; mix well. Spread the mixture on the steak slices. Roll the steaks to enclose the filling, securing with wooden picks.

Heat the vegetable oil in a heavy skillet and add the steak rolls. Sauté for 3 to 5 minutes or until brown on all sides; drain. Add the water, marjoram and onion. Simmer, covered, for 30 minutes adding wine or water if needed for the desired consistency.

Serves 6

Bavarian Beef

1 pound ground beef
1 garlic clove, crushed
1 (16-ounce) can tomatoes
1 (8-ounce) can tomato sauce
2 teaspoons sugar
2 teaspoons salt
pepper to taste
5 ounces uncooked egg noodles
3 ounces cream cheese, chopped
1 cup sour cream
6 green onions, chopped
1 1/2 cups (6 ounces) shredded Cheddar cheese

Brown the ground beef in a saucepan, stirring until crumbly; drain. Add the garlic, undrained tomatoes, tomato sauce, sugar, salt and pepper and mix well. Simmer, covered, for 45 minutes.

Cook the noodles using the package directions; drain. Add the cream cheese and let stand to soften; mix well. Stir in the sour cream and green onions.

Preheat the oven to 350 degrees. Layer the ground beef mixture, noodle mixture and cheese in a 3-quart baking dish. Bake for 35 minutes.

Serves 4 to 6

Polka-Dot Potatoes and Beef

1 pound lean ground beef
2 (8-ounce) cans tomato sauce
1 (12-ounce) can corn kernels with
*   bell peppers, drained*
1/2 cup chopped onion
1 teaspoon sugar
1/2 teaspoon oregano
1/2 teaspoon garlic salt
1/2 teaspoon salt
1/4 teaspoon pepper
2 cups mashed cooked potatoes
1 cup (4 ounces) shredded Cheddar cheese

Preheat the oven to 350 degrees. Brown the ground beef in a skillet, stirring until crumbly; drain. Add the tomato sauce, corn, onion, sugar, oregano, garlic salt, salt and pepper and mix well.

Spoon the mixture into a 1¹/₂-quart baking dish. Dollop the mashed potatoes in polka dots over the top and sprinkle with the cheese. Bake for 25 to 30 minutes or until heated through.

Serves 4 to 6

Mexican Casserole

1 pound lean ground beef
1 large onion, chopped
1 (10-ounce) can tomatoes with green chiles
1 (16-ounce) can ranch-style beans
1 (10-ounce) can cream of chicken soup
1 garlic clove, minced, or 2 tablespoons
    prepared chopped garlic
1 tablespoon chili powder, or to taste
garlic salt to taste
1 package corn tortillas
2 cups (8 ounces) shredded Colby Jack cheese

Garnish: black olives, chopped fresh tomatoes
    and/or sour cream

Preheat the oven to 350 degrees. Brown the ground beef with the onion in a skillet, stirring until crumbly; drain.

Combine the tomatoes with green chiles, beans, soup, garlic, chili powder and garlic salt in a saucepan. Bring to a simmer, stirring to mix well; remove from the heat. Stir into the ground beef mixture.

Tear the tortillas into quarters. Layer the tortilla pieces, ground beef mixture and cheese 1/2 at a time in a lightly greased 9×13-inch baking dish.

Bake for 30 minutes or until the layers are heated through and the cheese is melted and bubbly. Garnish with black olives, tomatoes and sour cream. Serve with tortilla chips.

Serves 8

Manicotti

1 pound ground beef
1 (16-ounce) package manicotti noodles
salt to taste
vegetable oil
2 eggs, beaten
2 cups ricotta cheese
1/2 cup (2 ounces) grated Parmesan cheese
4 cups (16 ounces) shredded mozzarella cheese
Italian seasoning, seasoned salt and pepper to taste
1 (48-ounce) jar spaghetti sauce or
    Homemade Spaghetti Sauce (page 82)

Preheat the oven to 350 degrees. Brown the ground beef in a skillet, stirring until crumbly; drain. Cook the manicotti noodles with salt and a small amount of oil in water in a saucepan for 3 minutes; drain.

Combine the ground beef with the eggs, ricotta cheese, Parmesan cheese and 1/3 of the mozzarella cheese in a bowl and mix well. Season with Italian seasoning, seasoned salt and pepper. Spread a layer of spaghetti sauce in a 9×13-inch baking dish sprayed with nonstick cooking spray. Spoon the ground beef mixture into the noodles by hand or using a pastry bag. Arrange in a single layer in the prepared baking dish.

Spoon the remaining spaghetti sauce over the noodles and sprinkle with the remaining mozzarella cheese. Cover loosely with foil and bake for 45 minutes or until heated through.

Serves 6 to 8

Homemade Spaghetti Sauce

1 (20-ounce) package Italian sausage,
*   about 5 links, sliced*
2 to 3 tablespoons olive oil
1/4 to 1/2 cup chopped onion
3 garlic cloves, minced
2 pounds ground beef
8 ounces mushrooms, sliced
basil, oregano and garlic powder to taste
salt and pepper to taste
2 (28-ounce) cans crushed tomatoes
1 (28-ounce) can diced tomatoes
2 (15-ounce) cans tomato sauce
1 or 2 (6-ounce) cans tomato paste
1/4 to 1/3 cup sugar, or to taste

Remove the sausage from the casings and crumble. Heat the olive oil in a large saucepan. Add the onion and garlic and sauté for 4 to 5 minutes or until tender. Add the sausage and beef and cook until brown and crumbly, adding the mushrooms, basil, oregano, garlic powder, salt and pepper as the meat cooks.

Simmer until the mushrooms are tender; drain. Add the tomatoes, tomato sauce and tomato paste. Simmer for 1 hour. Stir in the sugar.

Serves 15

Spaghetti Carbonara

1 pound sliced bacon
8 ounces sliced Canadian bacon
1 pound Italian sausage
3 envelopes Alfredo sauce mix
1 green onion, chopped (optional)
1/2 cup sliced mushrooms (optional)
1/2 cup frozen peas (optional)
16 ounces uncooked spaghetti

Cut the bacon and Canadian bacon into 1-inch pieces. Remove the casings from the Italian sausage and crumble. Cook the meats in a skillet, stirring until the sausage and Canadian bacon are brown and the bacon is crisp; remove to a bowl, reserving the drippings in the skillet. Keep the bacon mixture warm in a low oven.

Prepare the Alfredo sauce using the package directions. Sauté the green onion, mushrooms and peas in the reserved drippings in the skillet; drain. Return the bacon mixture to the skillet and add the Alfredo sauce; mix well. Simmer until heated through.

Cook the spaghetti using the package directions; drain. Spoon into a large bowl and pour the sauce mixture over the top; stir to coat well. Serve with a green salad and warm garlic bread.

Serves 8

Jalapeño-Stuffed Pork Tenderloin

2 peppercorn-marinated pork tenderloins
8 ounces goat cheese
2 or 3 jalapeño chiles, seeded and chopped
1 pound sliced bacon

Preheat the oven to 350 degrees. Butterfly the pork tenderloins and lay flat on a work surface. Mix the goat cheese and jalapeño chiles in a small bowl. Spread on the cut sides of the pork and replace the sides to enclose the cheese mixture. Wrap the tenderloins with the bacon.

Place in a roasting pan sprayed with nonstick cooking spray. Roast for 20 minutes. Increase the oven temperature to broil and broil the tenderloins for 5 to 7 minutes. Slice and serve with Apple Jelly Sauce.

Serves 6 to 8

Apple Jelly Sauce

2 (8-ounce) jars apple jelly
2 (8-ounce) jars pineapple jelly
2 teaspoons creamy prepared horseradish
1 tablespoon freshly ground pepper

Combine the apple jelly, pineapple jelly, horseradish and pepper in a small saucepan and mix well. Simmer until heated through, stirring frequently. Serve with pork or venison.

Serves 16

Marinated Pork Tenderloin

1/2 cup soy sauce
3 tablespoons sugar
2 tablespoons minced onion
2 garlic cloves, minced
2 teaspoons ginger
1/2 to 3/4 cup sesame seeds
2 tablespoons vegetable oil
2 pork tenderloins, about 2 pounds, trimmed
Raspberry Mustard Sauce (optional, below)

Combine the soy sauce, sugar, onion, garlic, ginger and sesame seeds in a shallow dish. Add the vegetable oil and mix well. Add the pork tenderloins, turning to coat evenly. Marinate in the refrigerator for 8 hours or longer; drain.

Preheat the oven to 375 degrees. Place the tenderloins in an oiled broiler pan. Roast for 30 minutes. Let stand for 10 to 15 minutes. Slice 1/2 inch thick and serve with Raspberry Mustard Sauce.

Serves 4 to 6

Raspberry Mustard Sauce

1 (18-ounce) jar raspberry jelly
1 tablespoon spicy mustard
salt to taste

Melt the jelly in a small saucepan. Add the mustard, stirring to mix well. Stir in the salt and heat until bubbly. Serve with pork.

Makes 2 cups

Sour Cream Pork Chops

3/4 to 1 cup all-purpose flour
3 to 4 tablespoons paprika
1/2 teaspoon garlic powder
2 teaspoons pepper
6 thick-cut boneless pork chops

vegetable oil
1 large onion, cut into 6 slices
1 (10-ounce) can beef bouillon
2 cups sour cream

Preheat the oven to 375 degrees. Combine the flour, paprika, garlic powder and pepper in a plastic bag. Add the pork chops and shake to coat well. Heat a small amount of vegetable oil in a skillet. Add the pork chops and brown for 5 minutes on each side. Top each chop with an onion slice and remove to a 9×13-inch baking dish.

Add 2 to 3 tablespoons of the flour mixture remaining in the plastic bag to the drippings in the skillet and cook for 2 to 3 minutes, stirring to blend well. Add the beef bouillon and cook until smooth and thickened, stirring constantly.

Stir in the sour cream and pour over the pork chops. Bake, covered, for 1 to 1 1/4 hours or until done to taste. Serve with buttered noodles.

Serves 6

It's Showtime

In the spring of 1980, the Junior League voted to take on its first major project: helping to bring a performing arts facility to Waco. With an initial grant of $55,000 and a ten-year commitment—the League's largest financial gift and pledge of support ever at the time—the Waco Hippodrome opened its doors in 1986. It continues to set the stage for nationally-acclaimed Broadway musicals and a variety of musical performances for Central Texans to enjoy.

Sour Cream Chicken Enchiladas

1 (3-pound) chicken
1 jalapeño chile, cut into halves
1 sweet onion, cut into halves
4 tomatillos, chopped
5 garlic cloves, chopped
1 jalapeño chile, chopped
1 sweet onion, chopped
1 tablespoon olive oil
1/2 cup chopped fresh cilantro
2 teaspoons cumin
2 teaspoons salt
1 teaspoon pepper

24 corn tortillas
1 (20-ounce) can salsa verde
2 cups sour cream
1 (10-ounce) can cream of chicken soup
4 cups (16 ounces) shredded Monterey
   Jack cheese
1 cup (4 ounces) shredded
   Cheddar cheese

Garnish: cilantro, black olives, chopped
   tomatoes, guacamole and/or lettuce

Combine the chicken with the jalapeño chile halves and onion halves in enough water to cover the chicken. Cook for 1 hour or until the chicken is very tender and falling from the bone; drain. Shred the chicken, discarding the skin and bones.

Preheat the oven to 350 degrees. Sauté the tomatillos, garlic, chopped jalapeño chile and chopped onion in the olive oil in a sauté pan for 10 minutes, adding the cilantro at the end of the cooking time. Season with the cumin, salt and pepper. Combine with the chicken in a bowl and adjust the seasonings.

Dip the tortillas 1 at a time into the salsa verde or heat in the microwave to soften and place on a work surface. Spoon the chicken mixture onto the tortillas and roll to enclose the filling. Combine the remaining salsa verde with the sour cream and soup in a bowl and mix well.

Arrange the enchiladas in a 9×13-inch baking dish and pour the sauce mixture over the top; sprinkle with the cheeses. Bake for 30 minutes or until heated through. Garnish with cilantro, black olives, tomatoes, guacamole and/or lettuce.

Serves 12

Gourmet Chicken Spaghetti

1 (3-pound) chicken
8 ounces uncooked thin spaghetti
8 ounces fresh mushrooms
1/2 cup (1 stick) butter
1/4 cup all-purpose flour
1 cup cream
1 cup mayonnaise
1 cup sour cream
1 cup (4 ounces) grated
   Parmesan cheese

2 tablespoons lemon juice
1/4 cup white wine
1 teaspoon dry mustard
1/2 teaspoon garlic powder
1 teaspoon salt
1/2 teaspoon cayenne pepper
paprika to taste
grated Parmesan cheese to taste

Cook the chicken in enough water to cover in a large saucepan until tender. Remove the chicken, reserving the broth. Cool the chicken and cut into pieces, discarding the skin and bones. Cook the spaghetti in the reserved chicken broth; drain, reserving the spaghetti and 1 cup of the broth. Combine the chicken and spaghetti in a shallow 3-quart baking dish.

Preheat the oven to 350 degrees. Sauté the mushrooms in 1/4 cup of the butter in a saucepan. Add to the baking dish.

Melt the remaining 1/4 cup butter in a saucepan. Stir in the flour and cook until bubbly. Add the cream and the reserved 1 cup chicken broth. Cook until thickened, stirring constantly. Stir in the mayonnaise, sour cream, 1 cup Parmesan cheese, lemon juice, wine, dry mustard, garlic powder, salt and cayenne pepper.

Pour the sauce over the chicken and spaghetti in the baking dish. Sprinkle with paprika and additional Parmesan cheese. Bake for 30 to 40 minutes or until bubbly.

Serves 8

Champagne Chicken with Shrimp

1 cup sliced mushrooms
1 tablespoon extra-virgin olive oil
4 boneless skinless chicken breasts
1 1/2 cups Champagne
2 tablespoons minced shallots
2 plum tomatoes, chopped
3/4 cup heavy cream
salt and pepper to taste

3 garlic cloves, minced
2 tablespoons butter
12 large shrimp, peeled and deveined
8 ounces angel hair pasta, cooked
1/4 cup heavy cream
2 tablespoons freshly chopped rosemary
1 cup (4 ounces) grated
    Parmesan cheese

Sauté the mushrooms in the olive oil in a saucepan over medium heat until the liquid evaporates. Remove the mushrooms to a bowl with a slotted spoon and keep warm. Add the chicken to the saucepan and sauté until cooked through. Remove to the bowl and keep warm.

Add the Champagne to the saucepan and bring to a boil, stirring to deglaze the saucepan. Stir in the shallots and tomatoes and cook for 8 to 10 minutes or until the liquid is reduced to 1/2 cup. Stir in 3/4 cup cream and cook for 2 minutes. Return the mushrooms and chicken to the saucepan. Season with salt and pepper and keep warm over low heat.

Sauté the garlic in the butter in a large sauté pan over medium-high heat. Add the shrimp and sauté until cooked through. Toss the pasta with 1/4 cup cream and the rosemary in a bowl. Spoon the pasta onto serving plates and spoon the chicken and sauce over the pasta. Top with the shrimp and sprinkle with the Parmesan cheese.

Serves 4

Chicken Italian

4 boneless skinless chicken breasts
1 or 2 eggs, beaten
1 cup bread crumbs or cracker crumbs
$^1/_2$ cup olive oil

2 cups pizza sauce
1 to 2 cups (4 to 8 ounces) grated
  Parmesan cheese
4 slices mozzarella cheese

Preheat the oven to 350 degrees. Pound the chicken $^1/_4$ inch thick with a meat mallet. Dip into the eggs and coat with the bread crumbs. Brown on both sides in the olive oil in a skillet; drain.

Place the chicken in a baking dish and spoon the pizza sauce over the top. Sprinkle with the Parmesan cheese. Bake for 30 minutes. Top with the mozzarella cheese and bake for 10 minutes longer or until the cheese melts.

Serves 4

Chicken Jarlsberg

6 chicken breasts
$1^1/_3$ cups ($5^1/_3$ ounces) sliced
  Jarlsberg cheese
1 medium zucchini, thinly sliced
1 (10-ounce) can cream of
  mushroom soup

$^1/_4$ cup dry white wine
garlic powder, salt and pepper to taste
2 cups herb stuffing mix
$^1/_3$ cup melted butter

Preheat the oven to 350 degrees. Place the chicken in a 9×13-inch baking dish and top with the cheese and zucchini. Combine the soup and wine in a bowl and mix well. Spoon over the chicken; sprinkle with garlic powder, salt and pepper.

Sprinkle the stuffing mix over the chicken and drizzle with the melted butter. Bake for 30 to 35 minutes or until the chicken is cooked through.

Serves 6

Chicken Pie

Chicken Pie Pastry
1 1/2 cups all-purpose flour
1/2 cup (1 stick) butter
1/2 teaspoon salt
1/4 cup ice water

Pie
3 boneless skinless chicken breasts
1 cup heavy cream
1 (12-ounce) package frozen
    mixed vegetables

5 tablespoons unsalted butter
1 small yellow onion, chopped
5 tablespoons unbleached flour
1 cup chicken broth
1/4 cup dry white wine
1 1/2 teaspoons salt
1/2 teaspoon pepper
1 egg
1 tablespoon water

For the pastry, place the flour, butter and salt in a food processor. Process until the mixture resembles coarse meal. Add the ice water and process to form a ball. Wrap in plastic wrap and chill for 30 minutes.

For the pie, preheat the oven to 350 degrees. Arrange the chicken in a single layer in a baking pan and pour the cream over the top. Bake for 25 minutes. Remove the chicken, reserving the cream. Cool the chicken and cut into 1-inch pieces. Increase the oven temperature to 425 degrees.

Cook the frozen mixed vegetables partially, using the package instructions. Melt the butter in a saucepan and add the onion. Sauté for 5 minutes or until translucent. Stir in the flour and cook for 5 minutes, stirring constantly; do not brown. Add the chicken broth and cook until smooth and thickened, stirring constantly. Stir in the reserved cream and wine. Cook over low heat for 5 minutes. Season with the salt and pepper and add the mixed vegetables and chicken; mix gently. Pour into a 2-quart baking dish.

Roll the pastry into a circle 1 inch larger than the baking dish. Place over the filling, trim and press the overhanging pastry over the edge. Crimp the edge and brush with a wash of the egg and water. Cut a steam vent and place on a baking sheet. Place on the middle oven rack and bake for 20 to 25 minutes or until golden brown.

Serves 6

Parmesan Chicken Breasts

2 to 3 cups butter-flavor cracker crumbs
3/4 cup (3 ounces) grated
    Parmesan cheese
1/4 cup (1 ounce) grated Romano cheese
2 garlic cloves, crushed, or 1 teaspoon
    garlic powder

1/4 cup chopped fresh parsley
2 teaspoons salt
1/4 teaspoon pepper
12 boneless skinless chicken breasts
1 1/2 cups (3 sticks) butter, melted

Preheat the oven to 350 degrees. Combine the cracker crumbs, Parmesan cheese, Romano cheese, garlic, parsley, salt and pepper in a large plastic bag. Dip the chicken into the melted butter and place in the bag, shaking to coat evenly.

Place in a 9×13-inch baking dish. Drizzle with the remaining butter and sprinkle with the remaining crumb mixture. Bake for 1 to 1 1/2 hours or until the chicken is cooked through. You can substitute bread crumbs for the cracker crumbs and add 1 teaspoon Worcestershire sauce, 2 teaspoons prepared mustard and 2 teaspoons Italian seasoning, if desired.

Serves 12

Poppy Seed Chicken Casserole

4 chicken breasts, cooked and chopped
salt and pepper to taste
2 (10-ounce) cans cream of chicken soup
1 cup sour cream

2 teaspoons poppy seeds
1/2 cup (1 stick) margarine
1 roll butter crackers

Preheat the oven to 325 degrees. Place the chicken in a 9×11-inch baking dish and season with salt and pepper. Mix the soup with the sour cream in a small bowl. Spread over the chicken and sprinkle with the poppy seeds.

Melt the margarine in a saucepan and stir in the cracker crumbs. Sprinkle over the chicken and bake for 30 to 40 minutes. You can freeze this casserole, if desired.

Serves 4

Chicken Casserole with Rice and Vegetables

4 green onions, chopped
3 celery ribs, chopped
1 or 2 garlic cloves, finely minced
8 ounces fresh mushrooms, sliced
1/4 cup (1/2 stick) butter
2 cups cooked long grain and wild rice mix
1 (10-ounce) can cream of celery soup
1/2 cup mayonnaise
1 (16-ounce) can cut green beans, drained
1 (5-ounce) can sliced water chestnuts, drained
1 tablespoon Worcestershire sauce
Tabasco sauce to taste
salt and pepper to taste
4 cups chopped cooked chicken breasts
1/2 cup (2 ounces) grated Parmesan cheese
1 cup (4 ounces) shredded Monterey Jack cheese

Preheat the oven to 350 degrees. Sauté the green onions, celery, garlic and mushrooms in the butter in a saucepan until tender. Add the cooked rice and mix well.

Combine the soup, mayonnaise, green beans, water chestnuts, Worcestershire sauce, Tabasco sauce, salt and pepper in a large bowl. Add the rice mixture and chicken and mix well.

Spoon into a 9×13-inch baking dish and top with the Parmesan cheese and Monterey Jack cheese. Bake for 30 minutes or until bubbly.

Serves 8

Chicken Verde Stuffed Shells

2 fresh poblano chiles
2 pounds chicken breasts
2 tablespoons olive oil
1/2 cup chopped yellow onion
3 garlic cloves, minced
3 tablespoons chili powder
1 tablespoon cumin
1 teaspoon dried oregano
1/2 teaspoon salt
1 (11-ounce) can tomatillos, drained
   and finely chopped
1/2 bunch cilantro, chopped

1 jalapeño chile, seeded and minced,
   or to taste
1/2 (10-ounce) package frozen chopped
   spinach, thawed and drained
1 (10-ounce) can chicken broth
juice of 1 large lime
2 cups (8 ounces) shredded Mexican
   blend cheese
2 cups crema Mexicana
1 (16-ounce) package pasta shells
1 (8-ounce) jar green salsa

Preheat the oven to 400 degrees. Roast the poblano chiles until blistered; cool slightly and chop. Cut the chicken into bite-size pieces, discarding any skin and bones. Sauté the chicken in the olive oil in a saucepan until golden brown and cooked through. Add the onion and garlic and sauté until tender. Stir in the chili powder, cumin, oregano and salt. Add the tomatillos, cilantro, jalapeño chile and poblano chiles; mix well.

Stir in the spinach, chicken broth and lime juice. Simmer for 30 minutes. Remove from the heat and stir in 1 cup of the cheese and half the crema Mexicana. Let stand until cool or store in the refrigerator for up to 12 hours.

Cook the pasta shells using the package directions; drain. Fill with the chicken mixture. Mix the remaining crema Mexicana with the green salsa in a bowl. Spoon a thin layer of the mixture in a 6×9-inch baking dish. Layer half the pasta shells in the prepared dish and spread with half the remaining green salsa mixture and 1/2 cup of the remaining shredded cheese. Repeat the layers, using the remaining salsa mixture and cheese.

Bake the shells for 45 to 60 minutes or until heated through. You can also use the chicken and spinach filling for enchiladas, quesadillas or to spread on a pizza crust. You can substitute sour cream or Alfredo sauce for the crema Mexicana.

Serves 6

Chicken Tetrazzini

1/2 cup chopped green bell pepper
1 cup chopped onion
2 tablespoons butter
8 ounces spaghetti, cooked and drained
4 cups chopped cooked chicken
8 ounces mushrooms, sliced
2 (10-ounce) cans cream of
   mushroom soup

1 cup chicken broth
1/4 cup chopped pimento
3 cups (12 ounces) shredded
   Cheddar cheese
1/4 teaspoon celery salt
1/4 teaspoon salt
paprika

Preheat the oven to 350 degrees. Sauté the green bell pepper and onion in the butter in a saucepan. Add the spaghetti, chicken, mushrooms, soup, chicken broth, pimento and cheese. Season with the celery salt and salt and mix well.

Spoon into a greased large baking dish and sprinkle with paprika. Bake, covered, for 1 hour.

Serves 8

Let's Play

In 1987, the Junior League of Waco pledged its support and commitment to revitalize Cameron Park. To kick off this project, the League donated $50,000, which was matched by Waco Parks & Recreation, as its 50th anniversary gift to the community. The gift was used to build a state-of-the-art playground near the park clubhouse. "Anniversary Park" was one of Waco's first handicap-accessible playgrounds and has been enjoyed by community children ever since.

Chicken Fiesta

2 cups crushed Cheddar cheese crackers
2 tablespoons taco seasoning mix
5 chicken breasts, chopped
4 green onions, chopped
2 tablespoons melted butter
2 cups heavy cream
1 cup (4 ounces) shredded Monterey
   Jack cheese

1 cup (4 ounces) shredded
   Cheddar cheese
1/2 cup (2 ounces) shredded
   jalapeño cheese
1 (4-ounce) can chopped green chiles
1/2 teaspoon chicken bouillon granules

Preheat the oven to 350 degrees. Mix the cracker crumbs and taco seasoning mix in a plastic bag. Add the chicken and shake to coat well. Place in a greased 9×13-inch baking dish.

Sauté the green onions in the butter in a saucepan. Add the heavy cream, Monterey Jack cheese, Cheddar cheese, jalapeño cheese, green chiles and bouillon and mix well. Cook until the cheeses melt and the sauce is smooth.

Spoon the sauce over the chicken. Bake for 45 minutes or until the chicken is cooked through and the sauce is bubbly.

Serves 6

Getting Together for Kids

In 1987, the Junior League of Waco initiated collaboration between agencies and organizations that share the common mission of serving the youth in our area. The McLennan County Youth Collaboration (MCYC) was formed to encourage cooperation, coordination, and communication between the organizations; to identify and research the needs of youth; and to develop services to address these needs. Today, MCYC continues to be an advocate on behalf of youth in all aspects of their lives. The program has expanded to six counties, serving 7,000 children and seventy-one community organizations.

Mushroom Almond Chicken

2 (7-ounce) packages long grain and
    wild rice mix
1/2 cup milk
1/4 cup (1/2 stick) butter, melted
1 (10-ounce) can cream of
    mushroom soup
1 (10-ounce) can cream of celery soup

1 (10-ounce) can cream of chicken soup
11/2 cups sliced mushrooms
1 cup chopped celery
3 cups chopped uncooked chicken
2 cups (8 ounces) grated Parmesan cheese
8 ounces slivered almonds
1/2 cup white wine

Preheat the oven to 250 degrees. Mix the uncooked rice, milk and melted butter in a bowl. Spread in a buttered 9×13-inch baking dish. Combine the soups, mushrooms and celery in a bowl and mix well. Spread 2/3 of the soup mixture over the rice. Sprinkle the chicken in the dish and spread the remaining soup mixture over the chicken. Sprinkle with the Parmesan cheese and almonds. Bake for 2 hours. Pour the wine over the top and increase the oven temperature to 310 degrees. Bake for 30 minutes longer.

Serves 8 to 10

Mushroom Stuffing

1/2 cup chopped shallots
2 tablespoons olive oil
1 tablespoon chopped garlic
salt and white pepper to taste
21/2 to 3 ounces each portobello,
    crimini and shiitake mushrooms

juice of 1 lemon
11/2 tablespoons finely chopped
    fresh rosemary
2 tablespoons chopped fresh thyme
1/2 cup madeira
1 or 2 teaspoons honey

Sauté the shallots in the olive oil in a large skillet over medium heat. Add the garlic and sauté, stirring constantly to prevent burning. Season with salt and white pepper. Chop the mushrooms separately into uniform pieces. Add the portobello mushrooms to the skillet and sauté briefly; season with salt and white pepper. Add the remaining mushrooms and season. Sauté until the liquid evaporates. Stir in the lemon juice, rosemary and thyme. Add the wine and cook until the liquid has nearly evaporated. Stir in the honey and adjust the seasoning.

Makes enough to stuff 2 turkey breasts

Shallot and Mushroom-Stuffed Turkey Breasts with Madeira Sauce

Turkey Glaze
1/3 cup lemon juice
1/3 cup honey
2 tablespoons chopped fresh rosemary
salt and pepper to taste

Turkey
2 (2-pound) turkey breasts with bone
    and skin
salt and white pepper
Mushroom Stuffing (page 97)
olive oil

Madeira Sauce
3/4 cup madeira
1 cup heavy cream
salt and white pepper to taste

For the glaze, mix the lemon juice, honey and rosemary in a bowl and season with salt and pepper.

For the turkey, preheat the oven to 350 to 375 degrees. Remove the bone and tenderloin from the turkey breasts. Place each breast skin side up on a cutting board and cut a pocket through the thickest portion, leaving the top, bottom and opposite side intact.

Sprinkle the pockets generously with salt and white pepper. Spoon the Mushroom Stuffing into the pockets. Close the pockets to completely enclose the filling and secure in 4 or 5 places with twine.

Brush the glaze over the turkey and sprinkle generously with salt and white pepper. Heat a skillet over medium-high heat. Add enough olive oil to cover the bottom and heat. Add the turkey and sear until golden brown on all sides.

Remove to a baking sheet covered with baking parchment and brushed lightly with olive oil. Bake for 25 to 30 minutes or until the pan juices run clear and the thickest portion does not yield to the touch. Let stand, covered with foil, for 5 minutes.

For the sauce, cook the wine in a small saucepan until reduced by 1/2. Add the cream and whisk to mix well. Heat until bubbly and season with salt and white pepper.

Slice each turkey roll into 4 portions and drizzle with the sauce. You can also serve the sauce over bread pudding.

Serves 8

Barbecued Dove

12 slices jalapeño chile
12 dove breasts, boned
12 slices bacon

Preheat coals in a grill. Soak wooden picks in water for 5 minutes. Place the jalapeño chile slices inside the dove cavities and wrap each breast in a crisscross pattern with the bacon; secure with the wooden picks. Grill until done to taste.

Serves 4

Coca-Cola® Barbecue Sauce

1 (12-ounce) can Coca-Cola®
3 tablespoons orange juice
2 tablespoons soy sauce
1/4 cup vegetable oil
2 tablespoons grated orange zest
1 tablespoon freshly grated ginger
2 garlic cloves, minced
salt and pepper to taste

Combine the cola, orange juice, soy sauce and vegetable oil in a bowl and mix well. Add the orange zest, ginger, garlic, salt and pepper. Use as a marinade and grilling sauce for chicken, pork and game.

Makes 2 cups

Cornish Game Hens

6 Cornish game hens
olive oil
salt and pepper to taste
1/2 cup apple jelly or guava jelly
2/3 cup sauterne
1/4 cup orange juice
1 pound seedless red grapes, cut into halves

Garnish: *seedless red grapes*

Preheat the oven to 350 degrees. Brush the hens with olive oil and season generously with salt and pepper. Place in a baking pan and roast for 50 to 55 minutes or until the juices run clear, brushing occasionally with olive oil.

Combine the jelly, wine and orange juice in a saucepan, whisking until smooth. Cook until heated through. Stir in the grapes. Spoon into a sauce boat.

Place the hens on a serving platter and garnish with additional grapes. Serve with the sauce.

Serves 6

The Art of Learning

To address the needs of the learning disabled in the Waco community, the Learning Disabilities Task Force was organized in 1990. Through volunteer and financial support by the Junior League of Waco, these needs were met through the establishment of the Learning Disabilities Association of McLennan County, the support of two community workshops with nationally-recognized speakers, and the creation of a teacher manual distributed to teachers across McLennan County.

Quail in Mushroom Sauce

12 quail or dove
salt and pepper to taste
all-purpose flour
vegetable shortening

1 (10-ounce) can cream of
   mushroom soup
1 (10-ounce) can cream of chicken soup
2 tablespoons milk

Season the quail with salt and pepper and coat with flour. Brown in a small amount of vegetable shortening in a Dutch oven. Remove to a plate and drain the pan drippings.

Combine the mushroom soup, chicken soup and milk in a bowl and mix well. Return the quail to the Dutch oven and pour the soup mixture over the top. Simmer, covered, over low heat for 1 hour, stirring frequently.

Serves 6

Cajun Salmon

3 tablespoons olive oil
2 tablespoons lemon juice
3 garlic cloves, minced

1 tablespoon Cajun seasoning
salt and pepper to taste
1 pound salmon fillet

Combine the olive oil, lemon juice, garlic, Cajun seasoning, salt and pepper in a shallow dish and mix well. Add the salmon and marinate in the refrigerator for 1 hour or longer.

Preheat the oven to 350 degrees. Place the salmon on a baking pan and bake for 20 minutes.

Serves 3

Cedar Plank Salmon with Potlatch Seasoning

1 cedar plank
4 coriander seeds
2 teaspoons dried basil
2 teaspoons dried oregano
2 teaspoons paprika
4 teaspoons kosher salt
3 tablespoons crushed red pepper
2 teaspoons black pepper
1/2 cup olive oil
1 (2-pound) salmon fillet

Garnish: 1 lemon, cut into wedges

Soak the cedar plank in water for 5 to 6 hours. Combine the coriander seeds, basil, oregano, paprika, kosher salt, crushed red pepper and black pepper in a bowl. Add the olive oil and mix well for the marinade. Place the salmon in a sealable plastic bag and add the marinade. Marinate in the refrigerator for 1 to 2 hours.

Preheat a grill. Drain the cedar plank and heat on the grill for 5 minutes on each side. Remove the salmon from the marinade and place on the cedar plank. Grill for 20 to 25 minutes or until the fish is cooked through. Cut into servings and garnish with lemon wedges.

The cooking time can vary based on the thickness of both the plank and the salmon. Cedar planks can be found at gourmet shops and lumber suppliers. The marinade seasoning is good on any fish.

Serves 8 to 10

Pasta with Scallops

1 bunch green onions, chopped
1 garlic clove, minced
2 to 3 tablespoons olive oil
1 pound bay scallops
2 tablespoons oyster sauce

1 tablespoon finely chopped parsley
1 teaspoon oregano
16 ounces dried pasta

Garnish: *parsley sprigs*

Sauté the green onions and garlic in the olive oil in a medium skillet over medium-high heat until the green onions are tender. Add the scallops and sauté for 2 to 3 minutes. Stir in the oyster sauce, parsley and oregano. Simmer for 15 minutes.

Cook the pasta using the package directions; drain, rinse with hot water and drain again. Toss with the scallop mixture in a bowl. Spoon onto a large serving platter and garnish with sprigs of parsley. Serve immediately.

Serves 4

Crab Cakes

1 egg
1/2 cup mayonnaise
1 teaspoon Old Bay seasoning
1/8 teaspoon Italian oregano
1/8 teaspoon crushed red pepper
1/2 cup panko (Japanese bread crumbs)

1 pound lump crab meat
1 red bell pepper, finely chopped
1/2 green bell pepper, finely chopped
1/2 teaspoon lemon juice
1/4 teaspoon grated lemon zest

Preheat the oven to 450 degrees. Combine the egg with the mayonnaise in a bowl and mix well. Add the Old Bay seasoning, oregano, crushed red pepper and bread crumbs. Add the crab meat, bell peppers, lemon juice and lemon zest and mix well.

Shape the mixture into 6 cakes and place on a baking sheet sprayed with nonstick cooking spray. Bake for 25 minutes, turning after 10 minutes. Serve with rémoulade sauce or on a bed of mixed field greens.

Serves 3

Cheesy and Spicy Shrimp

1 pound shrimp or crab meat
salt and pepper to taste
8 ounces mushrooms, sliced
1/4 cup (1/2 stick) butter

1 (6-ounce) roll jalapeño cheese
1 (10-ounce) can cream of
  mushroom soup
1 (2-ounce) jar chopped pimento

Cook the shrimp with salt and pepper to taste in boiling water in a saucepan for 3 to 4 minutes. Drain, peel and devein the shrimp. Sauté the mushrooms in the butter in a small skillet.

Melt the cheese in a double boiler over simmering water or a heavy saucepan. Stir in the soup, mushrooms, pimento and shrimp. Season with salt and pepper. Cook until very hot. Serve over cooked rice or noodles.

You can also spoon this into individual ramekins, top with bread crumbs and broil until golden brown to serve as an elegant first course.

Serves 4

Shrimp Creole

2 medium onions, sliced
1 green bell pepper, cut into strips
1/2 cup olive oil
2 tablespoons all-purpose flour
2 (14-ounce) cans diced tomatoes
6 tablespoons tomato sauce

1 teaspoon oregano
1/2 teaspoon salt
1/4 teaspoon pepper
1 pound shrimp, peeled and deveined
hot cooked rice

Sauté the onions and green bell pepper in the heated olive oil in a skillet until tender. Stir in the flour and cook until smooth. Add the tomatoes, tomato sauce, oregano, salt and pepper and cook until thickened, stirring constantly. Cook over low heat until of the desired consistency.

Add the shrimp. Cook just until heated through. Serve over hot cooked rice.

Serves 4

Shrimp with Grits and Roasted Peppers

2 tablespoons butter
3 green onions, chopped
3 garlic cloves, chopped
2 teaspoons chopped fresh rosemary
1 cup quick-cooking grits
3^1/2 cups low-sodium chicken broth
3 tablespoons heavy cream
2 teaspoons hot red pepper sauce
1 teaspoon salt
^{1}/2 teaspoon pepper
1 large red bell pepper, roasted and chopped
1 large yellow bell pepper, roasted and chopped
30 large peeled shrimp
1 cup crumbled goat cheese

Preheat the oven to 400 degrees. Melt the butter in a large saucepan over medium heat. Add the green onions, garlic and rosemary and sauté for 2 minutes. Add the grits and sauté for 1 minute. Whisk in the chicken broth and cream. Simmer for 8 minutes or until the liquid is absorbed and the grits are thick and tender, stirring occasionally.

Whisk in the hot sauce, salt and pepper. Fold in the roasted bell peppers. Spoon into a buttered 7×11-inch baking dish. Press the shrimp in a single layer over the grits and sprinkle with the cheese.

Bake for 20 minutes or until the grits are heated through, the shrimp are opaque and the cheese is golden brown.

Serves 6

Shellfish Crepes in Wine Cheese Sauce

Crepes
4 eggs
2 cups all-purpose flour
1/4 cup (1/2 stick) butter or
   margarine, melted
1 cup milk
1 cup cold water
1/2 teaspoon salt

Shellfish Filling
1/4 cup (1/2 stick) butter
2 cups chopped cooked shrimp,
   about 1 pound
1 cup fresh crab meat or lobster,
   about 8 ounces

2 scallions, minced
1/4 cup dry vermouth or clam juice
1/8 teaspoon salt
1/8 teaspoon pepper
2 cups Wine Cheese Sauce (page 107)

Assembly
1/2 tablespoon melted butter or
   margarine
2 cups Wine Cheese Sauce (page 107)
2 cups (8 ounces) shredded Swiss cheese
1/4 cup (1/2 stick) butter or
   margarine, chopped

Garnish: 2 scallions, sliced

For the crepes, combine the eggs, flour, butter, milk, water and salt in a blender or food processor and process until smooth, scraping down the sides. Cover and chill for 1 hour.

Heat a lightly greased nonstick 8-inch skillet over medium heat. Add 3 tablespoons of the batter at a time, tilting the skillet to coat the bottom of the skillet evenly. Cook for 1 minute or until the crepe can be shaken loose from the skillet. Turn the crepe over and cook for 30 seconds. Stack the crepes between waxed paper.

For the filling, melt the butter in a large skillet over medium-high heat. Add the shrimp, crab meat and scallions and sauté for 1 minute. Stir in the wine, salt and pepper. Bring to a boil and cook for 7 minutes or until most of the liquid evaporates. Remove from the heat. Add 2 cups of the Wine Cheese Sauce and mix well.

To assemble and bake, drizzle 1/2 tablespoon melted butter into a 9×13-inch baking dish. Spoon about 3 tablespoons of the filling down the center of each crepe and roll the crepe to enclose the filling. Arrange the crepes seam side down in the prepared baking dish. Spoon the remaining Wine Cheese Sauce over the crepes and sprinkle with the Swiss cheese; dot with 1/4 cup butter. Cover and chill for 3 hours. Let stand at room temperature for 30 minutes. Preheat the oven to 450 degrees. Bake the crepes for 20 minutes or until heated through. Garnish with the sliced scallions.

Serves 8

Wine Cheese Sauce

1/4 cup cornstarch
1/4 cup milk
1/3 cup dry vermouth or clam juice
3 cups heavy cream

1/4 teaspoon salt
1/4 teaspoon pepper
2 cups (8 ounces) shredded
    Swiss cheese

Whisk the cornstarch into the milk in a small bowl. Bring the wine to a boil in a saucepan and cook until reduced to 1 tablespoon. Whisk into the cornstarch mixture. Combine with the cream, salt and pepper in the saucepan and mix well. Cook over medium-high heat for 2 minutes or until the mixture comes to a boil, whisking constantly. Cook for 1 minute or until thickened, continuing to whisk.

Add the Swiss cheese and reduce the heat. Simmer for 1 minute or until the sauce is smooth and the cheese melts, whisking constantly.

Makes 4 cups

Red Pepper and Garlic Shrimp

1 large garlic bulb
2 tablespoons butter
1/4 cup olive oil
1/2 cup dry white wine
1 tablespoon lemon juice
1 teaspoon dried oregano

10 dried red chile peppers
1/2 teaspoon crushed red pepper flakes
1 teaspoon salt
1 pound medium shrimp,
    peeled with tails intact

Cut the garlic bulb into halves crosswise; separate and peel the cloves. Melt the butter with the olive oil in a skillet and add the garlic cloves. Sauté for 2 minutes. Stir in the wine, lemon juice, oregano, chile peppers, crushed red pepper flakes and salt. Simmer over very low heat for 5 minutes. You can prepare the dish to this point in advance.

Add the shrimp and simmer for 5 to 6 minutes or just until the shrimp turn pink. Serve with Mexican rice and sautéed vegetables. You can remove the dried chile peppers to serve, as they are too hot for most people.

Serves 4

Veal Scallops in Lemon Sauce

Veal
1 teaspoon dried tarragon
1/4 cup dry white wine
1 cup Italian bread crumbs
1/2 cup (2 ounces) grated
    Parmesan cheese
1 teaspoon dried tarragon
1/2 teaspoon garlic powder
1/2 teaspoon seasoned salt
1/2 teaspoon freshly cracked pepper
1/2 cup (1 stick) butter
1 pound thinly sliced veal scallops
1 lemon, thinly sliced
3 tablespoons chopped parsley

Lemon Sauce
1 egg yolk
2 tablespoons white wine
2 tablespoons lemon juice
2 tablespoons butter
1 teaspoon dried tarragon

For the veal, soak 1 teaspoon tarragon in the wine in a cup. Mix the bread crumbs, Parmesan cheese, 1 teaspoon tarragon, garlic powder, seasoned salt and pepper in a shallow bowl. Melt the butter in a large skillet.

Coat the veal lightly with the bread crumb mixture and add to the skillet. Sauté until brown on both sides. Stir in the wine and tarragon mixture, lemon slices and parsley. Simmer for 10 minutes. Remove to a warm platter, discarding the lemon slices, and keep warm.

For the sauce, beat the egg yolk with the wine and lemon juice in a bowl. Melt the butter in a medium skillet and add the egg yolk mixture. Stir in the tarragon. Cook over low heat until the desired consistency, stirring constantly. Serve over the veal.

Serves 6

Eggplant Parmesan

2 eggs
1 1/2 cups milk
1 package Italian-seasoned bread
    crumbs or Parmesan
    cheese-seasoned bread crumbs

2 large eggplant
olive oil or vegetable oil
1 (32-ounce) jar spaghetti sauce
2 cups (8 ounces) shredded
    mozzarella cheese

Preheat the oven to 350 degrees. Whisk the eggs and milk together in a bowl. Place the bread crumbs in a shallow dish. Peel the eggplant and cut into 1/4-inch slices. Dip the slices into the milk mixture and coat with the bread crumbs. Heat olive oil in a skillet and add the eggplant slices. Fry until the coating is crisp and golden brown and the eggplant is tender; drain.

Arrange half the slices in a single layer in a 9×13-inch baking dish. Spread with half the spaghetti sauce and sprinkle with half the mozzarella cheese. Repeat the layers. Bake until the layers are heated through and the cheese melts. Serve immediately with garlic bread.

Serves 8

Show on a String

Junior League of Waco's Drug Puppets Troupe began in 1990, presenting lively puppet shows to first-grade students throughout McLennan County each week for many years. With fun characters and engaging age-appropriate dialogue, the show creatively educated students about the dangers of substance abuse and demonstrated strategies to stay away from drugs and alcohol. More than 2,400 students from twenty-eight elementary schools enjoyed the performances each year.

Side Dishes

What's on the side? Veggies—all kinds.

The farmer's market has all the best finds.

Add rice or pasta to round out the plate.

If you're taking it somewhere, please don't be late!

This chapter graciously underwritten by Kelly, Realtors

Asparagus Vinaigrette

1 bunch fresh asparagus
3 tablespoons tarragon vinegar
10 tablespoons olive oil
2 tablespoons heavy cream
1 teaspoon Dijon mustard
$1/2$ teaspoon chopped garlic
2 teaspoons chopped parsley

$1/4$ teaspoon sugar
$1/2$ teaspoon dry mustard
1 teaspoon salt
$1/8$ teaspoon cayenne pepper
$1/2$ teaspoon black pepper
Worcestershire sauce and
    Tabasco sauce to taste

Cook the asparagus in a small amount of water in a saucepan until tender-crisp; drain. Combine the vinegar, olive oil, cream and Dijon mustard in a shallow dish. Add the garlic, parsley, sugar, dry mustard, salt, cayenne pepper and black pepper and mix well. Season with Worcestershire sauce and Tabasco sauce.

Add the asparagus to the vinaigrette mixture and coat evenly. Marinate in the refrigerator for 8 hours or up to 1 week.

Serves 4

Going Wild

Waco is home to the award-winning Cameron Park Zoo, a 52-acre natural habitat center for conservation, education, and recreation. The Junior League has a long, productive history with both the Cameron Park Zoo and its predecessor, the Central Texas Zoo. The League contributed more than $150,000 and countless volunteer hours to both zoos and started the first Zoo Education Program, in addition to purchasing the first "Zoomobile" for education outreach county programs. The League was instrumental in creating and participating in Zoo Adventure Camp, which is still a well-loved summer activity for children. In 2004, the League provided a $25,000 community gift to fund the creation of a new butterfly exhibit.

Brazos Baked Beans

1 pound bacon, cut up
1 large onion, chopped
1 medium green bell pepper, chopped
5 (16-ounce) cans pork and beans,
    drained
1 (14-ounce) bottle of ketchup

2$^{1}/_{2}$ cups packed brown sugar
$^{1}/_{4}$ teaspoon prepared mustard
$^{1}/_{4}$ cup Worcestershire sauce
2 teaspoons liquid smoke
Tabasco sauce to taste

Preheat the oven to 300 degrees. Cook the bacon until crisp in a large skillet. Add the onion and green bell pepper and sauté until tender; drain.

Combine the bacon and sautéed vegetables with the pork and beans, ketchup, brown sugar, mustard, Worcestershire sauce, liquid smoke and Tabasco sauce in a bowl and mix well. Spoon into a large baking dish and bake for 2 hours.

Serves 12

Beans à la Chara

8 ounces dried pinto beans
1 ($^{1}/_{2}$-inch-wide) slice salt pork
$^{1}/_{2}$ teaspoon oregano
1 tablespoon chili powder
salt and pepper to taste
4 slices bacon, chopped

1 large onion, chopped
2 garlic cloves, minced
1 tomato, chopped
1 poblano chile, seeded and chopped
2 tablespoons chopped cilantro

Combine the beans with enough water to cover in a medium saucepan; let soak for 2 hours. Add the salt pork and bring to a boil over medium heat. Reduce the heat and cover; simmer for 1$^{1}/_{2}$ to 2 hours or until the beans are partially tender. Stir in the oregano, chili powder, salt and pepper.

Sauté the bacon with the onion, garlic, tomato, poblano chile and cilantro in a skillet for 10 minutes. Add to the beans and simmer for 30 minutes longer or until the beans are tender. Serve with fajitas.

Serves 8

Bean Bake with Sausage

1 pound bulk pork sausage
1 (16-ounce) can dark red kidney beans
1 (16-ounce) can black beans
1 (16-ounce) can navy beans
1 (16-ounce) can pinto beans
1 (31-ounce) can pork and beans
1/2 cup packed brown sugar
1/2 cup barbecue sauce
1/2 cup ketchup
1/2 large onion, chopped
1 (10-ounce) can tomatoes with green chiles
1 teaspoon liquid smoke
1 teaspoon prepared mustard
1/2 teaspoon salt
1/2 teaspoon coarsely ground pepper
6 to 8 slices bacon

Preheat the oven to 450 degrees. Brown the sausage in a skillet, stirring until crumbly; drain. Combine with the kidney beans, black beans, navy beans, pinto beans and pork and beans in a large bowl; mix well.

Add the brown sugar, barbecue sauce, ketchup, onion, tomatoes with green chiles, liquid smoke, mustard, salt and pepper; mix well.

Spoon the bean mixture into a 9×13-inch baking dish. Arrange the bacon over the top. Bake for 1 hour. You can broil for several minutes if the bacon is not as crisp as desired. You can also prepare this dish in a slow cooker.

Serves 12

Bundles of Beans

2 (16-ounce) cans whole green beans, drained
4 slices bacon, cut into halves
1/2 cup packed brown sugar
1/4 cup (1/2 stick) butter, melted
1/2 garlic clove, crushed

Preheat the oven to 350 degrees. Divide the beans into 8 portions. Wrap each portion with 1/2 slice bacon and secure with a wooden pick. Arrange the bundles in a baking dish.

Combine the brown sugar, butter and garlic in a small bowl and mix well. Pour over the beans. Bake for 35 minutes.

Serves 8

Pennsylvania Dutch Green Beans

9 slices bacon
3 slices onion, separated into rings
3 (16-ounce) cans green beans
6 tablespoons cornstarch

3/4 teaspoon dry mustard
1 1/2 teaspoons salt
3 tablespoons vinegar
3 tablespoons brown sugar

Cook the bacon in a skillet until crisp; remove the bacon to a paper towel. Drain all but 3 tablespoons of the drippings from the skillet. Add the onion to the skillet and sauté over low heat.

Drain the liquid from the beans into a medium bowl. Add the cornstarch, dry mustard and salt to the liquid and whisk to blend well. Add to the skillet and cook until thickened, stirring constantly.

Mix the vinegar and brown sugar in a small bowl. Add to the skillet and mix well. Bring to a boil and reduce the heat. Stir in the beans and cook until heated through. Spoon into a large bowl and crumble the bacon over the top.

Serves 8

Sweet Carrot Soufflé

2 cups cooked sliced carrots
3 eggs
2 tablespoons all-purpose flour
1/2 cup sugar
1 cup milk
1/4 cup (1/2 stick) butter, softened
1/4 teaspoon cinnamon

Preheat the oven to 350 degrees. Combine the carrots, eggs, flour, sugar, milk, butter and cinnamon in a blender and process until smooth. Spoon into a 9×13-inch baking dish. Bake for 45 minutes or until set.

Serves 6

Cheese and Corn Casserole

1 (16-ounce) can cream-style corn
1 (16-ounce) can whole kernel corn, drained
8 ounces cream cheese, softened
1/2 cup milk
2 tablespoons butter
2 (4-ounce) cans chopped green chiles
1 cup (4 ounces) shredded cheese

Preheat the oven to 350 degrees. Combine the cream-style corn, whole kernel corn, cream cheese, milk, butter and green chiles in a saucepan. Cook over low heat until the cream cheese and butter melt, stirring to mix well.

Spoon into a lightly greased 2-quart baking dish and top with the cheese. Bake for 30 minutes or until bubbly. You can prepare the dish in advance and freeze until baking time.

Serves 8

Creamy Hominy Casserole

1 onion, chopped
1/2 cup chopped green bell pepper
3 tablespoons margarine
3 tablespoons all-purpose flour
1 teaspoon dry mustard
1/2 teaspoon salt
red pepper flakes to taste

1 1/2 cups milk
1 cup (4 ounces) shredded
    Cheddar cheese
1 (29-ounce) can hominy, drained
1 cup chopped green chiles
1/2 cup chopped black olives
1/2 cup bread crumbs

Preheat the oven to 350 degrees. Sauté the onion and green bell pepper in the margarine in a saucepan. Stir in the flour, dry mustard, salt and red pepper. Cook until bubbly. Add the milk gradually and cook over medium heat until thickened, stirring constantly. Add the cheese and cook until the cheese melts, stirring to mix well.

Remove from the heat and add the hominy, green chiles and black olives. Spoon into a 1 1/2-quart baking dish and top with the bread crumbs. Bake for 30 minutes.

Serves 6 to 8

Stuffed Red Peppers

4 red bell peppers
2 tablespoons balsamic vinegar
2 teaspoons olive oil
2 garlic cloves, minced
salt and pepper to taste
1 pound Roma tomatoes, chopped

1 cup (4 ounces) shredded
    mozzarella cheese
1/2 cup (2 ounces) grated
    Parmesan cheese
2/3 cup julienned and loosely packed
    fresh basil

Preheat the oven to 375 degrees. Cut the red bell peppers into halves lengthwise, discarding the seeds and membranes. Combine the balsamic vinegar, olive oil, garlic, salt and pepper in a bowl and whisk until smooth. Stir in the tomatoes, mozzarella cheese, Parmesan cheese and basil.

Spoon the tomato mixture into the pepper halves and arrange on a baking sheet sprayed with nonstick cooking spray. Bake for 40 minutes or until the peppers are tender.

Serves 8

Cheesy Potato Casserole

2 large potatoes, peeled and chopped
1/2 cup sour cream
3 ounces cream cheese, softened
2 tablespoons butter, softened
1/3 cup milk
1/4 cup (1 ounce) shredded
   Cheddar cheese
1/4 cup (1 ounce) shredded
   Muenster cheese

1 tablespoon salt, or to taste
1/2 teaspoon pepper
1 tablespoon butter, chopped

Garnish: *minced fresh chives,
   crumbled crisp-cooked bacon and/or
   shredded cheese*

Preheat the oven to 400 degrees. Cook the potatoes in enough boiling water to cover in a saucepan for 15 minutes or until tender; drain. Combine with the sour cream, cream cheese and 2 tablespoons butter in a mixing bowl. Beat at medium speed until smooth.

Stir in the milk, Cheddar cheese, Muenster cheese, salt and pepper. Spoon into a lightly greased 1-quart baking dish and dot with 1 tablespoon butter. Bake for 15 to 20 minutes or until heated through. Garnish with minced fresh chives, bacon or additional cheese.

You can easily triple the recipe or prepare it in advance and chill in the refrigerator for up to 8 hours. Let stand at room temperature for 30 minutes before baking.

Serves 2 to 3

Garlic and Blue Cheese Mashed Potatoes

5 pounds potatoes, peeled and chopped
1/2 cup (1 stick) butter
3 cups milk

2 tablespoons minced garlic
2 cups crumbled blue cheese

Cook the potatoes in enough water to cover in a saucepan until tender; drain and return to the saucepan. Add the butter and let stand until melted. Add the milk and garlic and mash with a hand masher until smooth. Mix in the blue cheese. Let stand for 5 minutes and stir before serving.

Serves 8

Roasted Potatoes with Goat Cheese

12 small red potatoes, quartered
4 shallots, roasted and quartered
2 garlic cloves, chopped
2 teaspoons chopped fresh rosemary
1 teaspoon chopped fresh oregano
kosher salt to taste
1 teaspoon crushed red pepper
2 teaspoons olive oil
1 tablespoon chopped fresh chives
1 red bell pepper, blanched and sliced
1 yellow bell pepper, blanched and sliced
1 bunch asparagus, blanched
4 ounces goat cheese

Garnish: lavender, rosemary and cracked pepper

Preheat the oven to 375 degrees. Combine the potatoes, shallots, garlic, rosemary, oregano, kosher salt and crushed red pepper in a bowl. Drizzle with the olive oil and toss gently to coat evenly.

Bake for 50 minutes or until tender. Add the chives and bell peppers and toss lightly. Arrange the asparagus around the edges of a platter and spoon the potato mixture onto the platter. Scoop the goat cheese into balls and scatter over the top. Garnish with lavender, rosemary and pepper.

Serves 4

Spinach and Artichoke Casserole

4 (10-ounce) packages frozen
  chopped spinach
11 ounces cream cheese, softened
juice of 1 lemon
5 tablespoons melted butter

nutmeg, seasoned salt, salt and pepper
  to taste
2 (16-ounce) cans artichoke hearts,
  drained

Preheat the oven to 350 degrees. Cook the spinach using the package directions; drain well. Combine the cream cheese with the lemon juice and butter in a bowl and mix until smooth. Add the spinach, nutmeg, seasoned salt, salt and pepper and mix well.

Arrange the artichoke hearts in a shallow baking dish. Spoon the spinach mixture over the artichokes. Cover tightly with foil and pierce holes in the foil. Bake for 30 minutes.

Serves 12

Garden Squash Casserole

1 red bell pepper
1 green bell pepper
1 1/2 pounds yellow squash, sliced
1 1/2 cups chicken broth
2 eggs, beaten

1 cup dry bread crumbs
4 ounces crumbled goat cheese
1 tablespoon lemon juice
1 teaspoon Dijon mustard

Preheat the oven to 375 degrees. Chop the bell peppers in a food processor. Combine with the squash and chicken broth in a saucepan and bring to a boil. Cook until the vegetables are tender; drain.

Combine the cooked vegetable mixture with the eggs, bread crumbs, goat cheese, lemon juice and Dijon mustard in a large bowl and mix well.

Spoon into an 8×8-inch baking dish sprayed with nonstick cooking spray. Bake for 35 to 40 minutes or until heated through.

Serves 6 to 9

Southern Sweet Potatoes

Pecan Topping (optional)
1¹/4 cups packed brown sugar
³/4 cup all-purpose flour
¹/2 cup (1 stick) butter, melted
1¹/2 cups chopped pecans

Sweet Potatoes
2 sweet potatoes, cooked and chopped
2 eggs

1 cup sugar
1 (5-ounce) can evaporated milk
¹/4 cup (¹/2 stick) butter
1 teaspoon cinnamon
1 teaspoon nutmeg
1 jigger (3 tablespoons) bourbon
miniature marshmallows

For the topping, mix the brown sugar, flour, butter and pecans in a bowl.

For the sweet potatoes, preheat the oven to 325 degrees. Mash the sweet potatoes in a bowl. Add the eggs, sugar, evaporated milk, butter, cinnamon and nutmeg and mix well. Spoon into a baking dish and bake for 30 to 45 minutes or until heated through.

Poke holes all the way through the mixture and pour the bourbon over the top. Add the topping and bake for 10 minutes. Sprinkle with marshmallows and bake just until the marshmallows are golden brown.

Serves 4

Cilantro and Lime Rice

2 cups chicken broth
1 cup uncooked rice
¹/2 cup chopped fresh cilantro

juice of 2 limes
2 tablespoons unsalted butter
¹/2 teaspon salt

Bring the chicken broth to a boil in a saucepan. Add the rice and reduce the heat to low. Simmer, covered, for 20 minutes or until the rice is tender and fluffy. Stir in the cilantro, lime juice, butter and salt.

Serves 4

Asparagus Risotto

12 ounces asparagus
salt to taste
3 tablespoons butter
1 tablespoon olive oil
1 tablespoon chopped scallion
1 1/2 cups uncooked arborio rice

1/2 cup dry white wine
1 garlic clove, minced
4 1/2 cups chicken stock
1/3 cup grated Parmesan cheese
4 ounces sliced prosciutto

Cook the asparagus in boiling salted water in a saucepan for 3 to 5 minutes or until tender-crisp. Drain and immerse in ice water to stop the cooking process; drain again. Cool to room temperature and cut into 1-inch pieces.

Melt the butter with the olive oil in a heavy saucepan over medium heat. Add the scallion and asparagus and sauté just until the scallion is tender; remove with a slotted spoon. Add the rice to the saucepan and sauté over medium heat for 1 minute, stirring with a wooden spoon until evenly coated. Add the wine and garlic and cook until the wine is absorbed.

Simmer the chicken stock in a saucepan. Add 4 1/4 cups of the stock to the rice, 1/2 cup at a time, cooking until almost completely absorbed after each addition; rice should be tender but still firm after about 20 minutes. Stir in the remaining 1/4 cup chicken stock. Remove from the heat and add the asparagus mixture and Parmesan cheese, mixing gently. Serve immediately with the prosciutto.

Serves 8

Children's Advocacy Center

In 1996, as its 60th anniversary gift to the community, the Junior League gave $100,000 to start the Advocacy Center for Crime Victims and Children. The center was created as a haven for victimized and abused children during the stressful investigation process. The Advocacy Center continues to provide a safe and comfortable place for frightened children to be interviewed and then helped to move on to happier, more secure lives.

Spanish Rice

1 cup uncooked rice
2 tablespoons bacon drippings or
    vegetable oil
1 medium onion, chopped
2 garlic cloves, chopped
1 (16-ounce) can stewed tomatoes
1 cup water

1 teaspoon cumin seeds
1/2 to 1 teaspoon oregano
1 teaspoon salt
1 teaspoon pepper
3/4 cup canned or cooked dried
    garbanzo beans (optional)

Sauté the rice in the bacon drippings in a saucepan until golden brown. Add the onion and garlic and sauté for 1 minute. Stir in the tomatoes, water, cumin seeds, oregano, salt and pepper.

Cover and simmer for 30 minutes. Stir in the garbanzo beans and simmer for 5 minutes longer or until the rice is tender and the liquid is absorbed.

Serves 4 to 6

Cheese and Garlic Grits

3 large garlic cloves, minced
2 teaspoons chopped fresh thyme
1 fresh New Mexico chile, chopped
1/4 cup (1/2 stick) butter
1 cup quick-cooking grits
1 (14-ounce) can chicken broth

1 (14-ounce) can beef broth
1/4 cup half-and-half
1/2 cup (2 ounces) shredded
    Muenster cheese
salt and pepper to taste
5 dashes of Tabasco sauce

Preheat the oven to 325 degrees. Sauté the garlic with the thyme and chile in the butter in a saucepan. Stir in the grits and cook for 1 minute. Stir in the chicken broth, beef broth and half-and-half. Cook until the liquid is absorbed, stirring occasionally.

Add the Muenster cheese, Tabasco sauce, salt and pepper and cook until the cheese melts, stirring to blend well. Spoon into a baking dish and bake for 30 minutes or until heated through.

Serves 4

Breads & Breakfast & Brunch

Wake up to muffins—warm and sweet.

Strawberry pancakes are always a treat.

Fresh-baked bread, homemade each day—

Be sure to give at least one loaf away!

This chapter graciously underwritten by Cargill Value Added Meats

Banana Bread

½ cup (1 stick) butter, softened
1½ cups sugar
2 eggs
2 ripe bananas, mashed
3 tablespoons milk

1 teaspoon vanilla extract
1¾ cups plus 1 teaspoon
   all-purpose flour
1 teaspoon baking soda

Preheat the oven to 350 degrees. Cream the butter and sugar in a mixing bowl until light and fluffy. Beat in the eggs, bananas, milk and vanilla. Add the flour and baking soda and mix well.

Spoon into a greased loaf pan and bake for 45 to 60 minutes or until the loaf tests done. You can also bake in miniature loaf pans, testing for doneness after 30 minutes.

Makes 1 loaf

Pumpkin Bread

1⅔ cups all-purpose flour
1¼ cups sugar
¼ teaspoon baking powder
1 teaspoon baking soda
½ teaspoon cinnamon
¼ teaspoon ground cloves
¼ teaspoon nutmeg

½ teaspoon salt
⅓ cup melted shortening
½ cup water
1 cup cooked pumpkin
2 eggs, beaten
⅓ cup chopped walnuts
⅔ cups raisins

Preheat the oven to 325 degrees. Sift the flour, sugar, baking powder, baking soda, cinnamon, cloves, nutmeg and salt into a bowl. Add the shortening, water, pumpkin, eggs, walnuts and raisins and mix well.

Spoon into a greased loaf pan and bake for 1¼ hours.

Makes 1 loaf

Lemon-Glazed Zucchini Pecan Bread

Bread
1 1/2 cups sifted all-purpose flour
1 1/2 teaspoons baking powder
1/4 teaspoon salt
1/3 cup margarine, softened
1 cup sugar
grated zest of 1 large lemon
2/3 cup shredded zucchini
2 eggs
1/2 cup milk
1/2 cup finely chopped pecans

Lemon Glaze
1/3 cup sugar
juice of 1 large lemon

For the bread, preheat the oven to 350 degrees. Sift the flour, baking powder and salt into a medium bowl. Cream the margarine and sugar with the lemon zest in a mixing bowl until light and fluffy. Mix in the zucchini and beat in the eggs 1 at a time.

Add the flour mixture alternately with the milk, ending with the flour and mixing well after each addition. Fold in the pecans. Spoon into a 5×9-inch loaf pan sprayed with nonstick cooking spray.

Bake for 45 to 50 minutes or until the loaf pulls away from the sides of the pan and a tester inserted into the center comes out clean. Place on a wire rack and pierce holes in the top with a fork.

For the glaze, blend the sugar and lemon juice in a small bowl. Drizzle evenly over the warm loaf and cool to room temperature. Loosen the edges of the bread from the pan with a spatula and invert onto a serving plate.

Makes 1 loaf

Strawberry Nut Bread

3 cups all-purpose flour
2 cups sugar
1 tablespoon cinnamon
1 teaspoon baking soda
1 teaspoon salt

4 eggs, beaten
1¼ cups vegetable oil
2 cups frozen sliced strawberries,
   thawed
1¼ cups chopped nuts

Preheat the oven to 350 degrees. Sift the flour, sugar, cinnamon, baking soda and salt into a mixing bowl; make a well in the center. Combine the eggs, vegetable oil, strawberries and nuts in a medium bowl. Add to the well in the dry ingredients and mix just until moistened.

Spoon into 2 greased 5×9-inch or six 3×6-inch loaf pans. Bake the larger loaves for 1 hour and the smaller loaves for 40 minutes. Cool in the pans for 10 to 15 minutes and remove to a wire rack to cool completely.

Makes 2 large loaves or 6 miniature loaves

Mexican Spoon Bread

1 cup yellow cornmeal
1 (16-ounce) can cream-style corn
⅓ cup corn oil, peanut oil or bacon
   drippings
¾ cup milk
2 eggs, beaten
½ teaspoon baking soda

1 teaspoon salt
2 (4-ounce) cans chopped green chiles,
   drained, or chopped jalapeño chiles
   to taste
1½ cups (6 ounces) shredded
   Cheddar cheese

Preheat the oven to 375 degrees. Combine the cornmeal, corn, corn oil, milk, eggs, baking soda and salt in a bowl and mix well. Spoon half the mixture into a greased 3-quart baking dish. Layer the green chiles and half the cheese over the batter.

Spoon the remaining batter over the cheese and top with the remaining cheese. Bake, covered with foil, for 45 to 50 minutes or until set and golden brown. Serve with taco salad or beef brisket.

Serves 6

Breads & Breakfast & Brunch

Oatmeal Banana Muffins

1/2 cup (1 stick) margarine, softened
1/2 cup sugar
2 eggs
3 medium bananas, mashed
3/4 cup honey
1 1/2 cups all-purpose flour
1 teaspoon baking powder
1 teaspoon baking soda
3/4 teaspoon salt
1 cup quick-cooking rolled oats

Preheat the oven to 375 degrees. Cream the margarine and sugar in a medium mixing bowl until light and fluffy. Beat in the eggs, bananas and honey.

Mix the flour, baking powder, baking soda and salt together in a bowl. Add to the banana mixture and mix just until moistened. Stir in the oats.

Spoon into greased or paper-lined muffin cups, filling 2/3 full. Bake for 18 to 20 minutes or until the muffins test done. Remove to wire racks to cool.

Makes 24

Cranberry Butter

1/2 cup (1 stick) butter, softened
1 1/2 cups confectioners' sugar
1 cup fresh or thawed frozen cranberries
1 teaspoon lemon juice

Combine the butter, confectioners' sugar, cranberries and lemon juice in a food processor fitted with a chopping blade. Process until the cranberries are chopped and the mixture is smooth. Serve with breads and muffins. Store in the refrigerator.

Makes 1 1/2 cups

Tangy Cranberry Orange Muffins

Muffins
2 cups all-purpose flour
2 teaspoons baking powder
1/2 cup sugar
3/4 teaspoon pumpkin pie spice
1/2 teaspoon ginger
1/2 teaspoon salt
1 egg
1/4 cup honey
3/4 cup vegetable oil
1/2 cup milk
grated zest of 2 oranges
1 (6-ounce) package dried cranberries, chopped

Orange Glaze
2 tablespoons melted butter
1 tablespoon honey
1 1/2 teaspoons Grand Marnier

For the muffins, preheat the oven to 400 degrees. Mix the flour, baking powder, sugar, pumpkin pie spice, ginger and salt in a bowl. Combine the egg, honey, vegetable oil and milk in a bowl and mix well. Whisk in the orange zest and dried cranberries. Add to the dry ingredients and mix just until moistened. Spoon into 12 paper-lined muffin cups. Bake for 20 minutes. Let stand at room temperature for 10 minutes.

For the glaze, combine the butter, honey and liqueur in a small bowl and mix well. Brush generously on the muffins. You can also serve with Cranberry Butter (page 129), if desired.

Makes 12

Healthy Morning Muffins

1¹/2 cups all-purpose flour or a mixture of
    all-purpose flour and whole wheat flour
1 cup raisin bran
³/4 cup Sugar Twin or Splenda
1 teaspoon baking powder
¹/2 teaspoon baking soda
1 teaspoon cinnamon
¹/2 teaspoon salt
²/3 cup peeled and shredded or
    finely chopped carrot
²/3 cup peeled and finely chopped apple
²/3 cup flaked coconut
²/3 cup raisins
²/3 cup chopped dates
²/3 cup chopped walnuts
1 egg
¹/2 cup egg substitute
¹/3 cup vegetable oil
1 cup unsweetened applesauce
1 teaspoon vanilla extract

Preheat the oven to 350 degrees. Mix the flour, raisin bran, Sugar Twin, baking powder, baking soda, cinnamon and salt together. Combine the carrot, apple, coconut, raisins, dates, walnuts, egg, egg substitute, vegetable oil, applesauce and vanilla in a large mixing bowl. Add the dry ingredients and mix just until moistened.

Spoon into muffin cups sprayed with nonstick cooking spray. Bake for 20 to 25 minutes or until a tester comes out clean. Serve with softened cream cheese.

Makes 24 to 30

Cheese Pull-Apart Bread

3 (12-count) packages frozen
   dinner rolls, thawed
   to room temperature
1/3 cup melted butter

1 cup (4 ounces) finely grated
   Parmesan cheese
1 cup (4 ounces) shredded
   provolone cheese

Roll each dinner roll in the butter and then in the Parmesan cheese, coating well. Arrange half the rolls in a greased 12-cup bundt pan. Sprinkle with the provolone cheese and add the remaining dinner rolls. Sprinkle with any remaining Parmesan cheese. Let rise for 1 hour or until doubled in bulk. Preheat the oven to 375 degrees. Bake the bread for 35 to 45 minutes or until golden brown, covering the edges with foil during the last 10 to 15 minutes if necessary to prevent overbrowning. Loosen the edge of the bread with a knife and invert onto a plate. Serve warm.

Serves 12

Cinnamon Pull-Apart Bread

Bread
1 cup granulated sugar
1 1/2 tablespoons cinnamon
2 cans refrigerator buttermilk biscuits
3/4 cup (1 1/2 sticks) butter or
   margarine, melted

Cream Cheese Glaze
4 ounces cream cheese, softened
1/2 cup confectioners' sugar
1 to 2 tablespoons milk

For the bread, preheat the oven to 350 degrees. Mix the granulated sugar and cinnamon in a bowl. Cut the biscuits into quarters with scissors. Roll in the cinnamon sugar mixture, coating evenly. Arrange half the biscuit pieces in a greased 12-cup bundt pan. Drizzle with half the butter. Repeat the layers with the remaining biscuits and butter. Sprinkle with any remaining cinnamon sugar mixture. Bake for 40 to 45 minutes or until golden brown. Invert onto a plate.

For the glaze, beat the cream cheese with the confectioners' sugar in a mixing bowl until smooth. Beat in enough milk to make the desired consistency. Spoon over the warm bread.

Serves 12

Focaccia

2¹/2 to 3 cups all-purpose flour
1 envelope dry yeast
2 teaspoons sugar
¹/4 cup olive oil
1 cup very warm water
¹/4 teaspoon salt
1 tablespoon olive oil
2 tablespoons Italian seasoning
2 tablespoons grated Parmesan cheese

For the standard method, mix 1 cup of the flour with the yeast, sugar, ¹/4 cup olive oil, water and salt in a bowl. Let stand for 3 minutes. Add enough additional flour to make an easily handled dough. Knead for 5 to 10 minutes or until smooth and elastic.

Place in a greased bowl, turning to coat the surface. Let rise for 1 to 1¹/2 hours or until doubled in bulk. Punch down the dough and divide into halves. Shape each into a flattened round 12-inch loaf on a baking stone or baking sheet lightly sprinkled with cornmeal. Let rise for 10 minutes.

Preheat the oven to 425 degrees. Prick the tops of the loaves with a fork and brush with 1 tablespoon of olive oil. Sprinkle with the Italian seasoning and Parmesan cheese. Bake for 12 to 15 minutes or until golden brown.

For the bread machine method, place the flour, yeast, sugar, ¹/4 cup olive oil, water and salt in the bread machine and start the machine using the dough setting. Punch down the dough when the cycle ends and proceed as above.

You can use a prepared Italian seasoning mix or make one using 1 teaspoon each of dried basil, dried oregano and dried rosemary mixed with ¹/2 teaspoon each of thyme, garlic powder and pepper.

Makes 2 loaves

Home-Baked Yeast Bread

1 envelope dry yeast
1¹/₄ cups warm (110- to
115-degree) water
2 tablespoons shortening, softened
2 tablespoons sugar
2 teaspoons salt
3 cups sifted all-purpose flour
melted butter

Dissolve the yeast in the warm water in a mixing bowl. Add the shortening, sugar, salt and half the flour. Beat at medium speed for 2 minutes or 300 vigorous strokes by hand, scraping the side of the bowl frequently. Add the remaining flour and mix with a spoon until smooth.

Scrape down the side of the bowl and cover with a towel. Let rise in an 85-degree place for 30 minutes. Beat 25 strokes and spoon into a loaf pan. Smooth the top and pat into shape with floured hands. Let rise for 40 minutes or until it rises to within 1 inch of the top edge of the loaf pan.

Preheat the oven to 375 degrees. Bake the bread for 45 to 50 minutes or until golden brown. Remove to a wire rack and brush with melted butter. Cool to room temperature before slicing.

Makes 1 loaf

Honey Rolls

Rolls
1 cup milk
1 egg
1 egg yolk
$^1/_2$ cup vegetable oil
2 tablespoons honey
$2^1/_2$ teaspoons dry yeast
$3^1/_2$ cups bread flour
$1^1/_2$ teaspoons salt

Honey Glaze
$^1/_3$ cup sugar
2 tablespoons melted margarine
1 tablespoon honey
1 egg white

For the rolls, heat the milk to 70 to 80 degrees in a saucepan. Combine with the egg, egg yolk, vegetable oil, honey, yeast, flour and salt in a bread machine. Use the dough setting to mix. Remove the dough to a greased bowl, turning to coat the surface. Let rise for 30 minutes. Shape into 24 small balls and arrange in a greased baking dish.

For the glaze, combine the sugar, margarine, honey and egg white in a bowl and mix well. Brush over the dough balls and allow to rise until doubled in bulk.

To bake, preheat the oven to 350 degrees. Bake the rolls for 20 to 25 minutes or until golden brown.

Makes 24

One-Hour Rolls

1 envelope dry yeast
$^1/_4$ cup warm water
2 cups all-purpose flour
2 tablespoons sugar
$^1/_2$ teaspoon baking powder
$^1/_4$ teaspoon baking soda
$^1/_2$ teaspoon salt
$^1/_4$ cup vegetable oil
$^3/_4$ cup buttermilk
melted butter

Dissolve the yeast in the water in a bowl. Sift the flour, sugar, baking powder, baking soda and salt into a bowl. Add the yeast mixture, vegetable oil and buttermilk and knead until smooth.

Roll $^1/_2$ inch thick on a floured surface and cut into rounds. Fold the rounds over and brush with melted butter. Arrange on a baking sheet and let rise in a warm place for 1 hour.

Preheat the oven to 425 degrees. Bake the rolls for 10 to 15 minutes or until golden brown.

Makes 24

Apple Cake

Cake
3 cups all-purpose flour
1 teaspoon baking soda
1 teaspoon salt
1 1/4 cups vegetable oil
2 cups sugar
3 eggs
1 1/2 teaspoons vanilla extract
3 cups sliced peeled red apples
1 1/2 cups chopped pecans or
    chopped walnuts

Brown Sugar Glaze
1 cup packed brown sugar
1/2 cup (1 stick) butter
1/4 cup heavy cream
1 teaspoon vanilla extract

For the cake, preheat the oven to 325 degrees. Sift the flour, baking soda and salt together. Combine the vegetable oil, sugar, eggs and vanilla in a large mixing bowl and mix well. Add the dry ingredients and mix until smooth. Stir in the apples and pecans.

Spoon the batter into a greased 9×13-inch cake pan. Bake for 1 hour.

For the glaze, combine the brown sugar, butter, cream and vanilla in a saucepan. Cook for 2 minutes or until the butter melts and the brown sugar dissolves, stirring constantly. Spoon over the hot cake in the pan. Serve for breakfast or brunch. You can store the cake for several days, as it will stay moist.

Serves 12

Gingerbread

2¹/2 cups all-purpose flour
1¹/2 teaspoons baking soda
1 teaspoon cinnamon
1 teaspoon ginger
1/2 teaspoon ground cloves
1/2 teaspoon salt
1 cup dark corn syrup
1 cup hot water
1/2 cup (1 stick) butter or shortening, softened
1/2 cup sugar
1 egg, beaten

Preheat the oven to 350 degrees. Sift the flour, baking soda, cinnamon, ginger, cloves and salt together. Blend the corn syrup and hot water in a small bowl. Cream the butter and sugar in a mixing bowl until light and fluffy. Beat in the egg.

Add the dry ingredients to the creamed mixture alternately with the syrup mixture, mixing until smooth after each addition.

Spoon into a 9×9-inch baking pan. Bake for 45 minutes or until a wooden pick inserted in the center comes out clean. Serve hot with Whipped Cream Sauce (below) or butter.

Serves 9

Whipped Cream Sauce

1 cup whipping cream
2 tablespoons honey, or
	3 tablespoons confectioners' sugar
1/2 teaspoon cinnamon

Whip the cream in a mixing bowl just until soft peaks form. Add the honey and cinnamon and whip until stiff peaks form. Chill in the refrigerator.

Makes 2 cups

Sour Cream Coffee Cake

Nut Filling
1/2 cup sugar
1/2 cup chopped nuts
1 teaspoon cinnamon

Cake
3 cups all-purpose flour
1 tablespoon baking powder

1 teaspoon baking soda
1/2 teaspoon salt
1 cup (2 sticks) butter, softened
1 cup sugar
3 eggs
1 cup sour cream
1 teaspoon vanilla extract

For the filling, mix the sugar, nuts and cinnamon in a bowl. Set aside for the filling.

For the cake, preheat the oven to 350 degrees. Mix the flour, baking powder, baking soda and salt together. Cream the butter and sugar in a mixing bowl until light and fluffy. Beat in the eggs. Add the dry ingredients to the creamed mixture alternately with the sour cream, mixing well after each addition. Mix in the vanilla.

Spoon half the mixture into a greased bundt pan. Sprinkle with half the nut filling mixture. Spread the remaining batter in the pan and top with the remaining filling.

Bake for 40 minutes or until a wooden pick inserted in the center comes out clean. Cool in the pan for several minutes and invert onto a plate to cool completely.

Serves 12

Hoopin' It Up

Tipped off by the Junior League, the City of Waco, the Waco Housing Authority, and the Waco Police Department, Moonlight Moves was a free co-ed basketball league for kids aged fifteen through twenty. The six-week summer program was held during the high-crime hours of 10 P.M. to 2 A.M. as a safe place where kids could hang out and stay away from trouble. Besides basketball, the program offered motivational and self-esteem training by local mentors and role models, and awarded new basketball shoes to those with perfect attendance. Moonlight Moves culminated in a basketball tournament at Baylor University's Ferrell Center.

Caramel French Toast

1½ cups packed brown sugar
6 tablespoons light corn syrup
¾ cup (1½ sticks) butter
10 thick slices French bread
4 eggs, beaten
2½ cups half-and-half

1 tablespoon vanilla extract
¼ teaspoon salt
3 tablespoons sugar
1½ teaspoons cinnamon
chopped pecans (optional)
¼ cup (½ stick) melted butter

Combine the brown sugar, corn syrup and ¾ cup butter in a medium saucepan. Cook over medium heat for 5 minutes or until bubbly, stirring constantly. Pour into a lightly greased 9×13-inch baking dish. Arrange the bread slices in the syrup.

Combine the eggs, half-and-half, vanilla and salt in a bowl and mix until smooth. Pour gradually over the bread slices. Chill, covered, for 8 hours or longer.

Preheat the oven to 350 degrees. Mix the sugar, cinnamon and pecans in a cup. Sprinkle evenly over the bread and drizzle with the melted butter. Bake, uncovered, for 45 minutes or until golden brown and bubbly.

Serves 8

A Pot of Gold

In 1999, the Junior League of Waco opened the Rainbow Room in the basement of the Raleigh Building in downtown Waco, home of Child Protective Services (CPS). When CPS removes a child from an abusive or neglectful situation, it sometimes happens suddenly and the child may have only the clothes he is wearing. The Rainbow Room is a resource for CPS caseworkers to meet the essential needs of those children, and is stocked with diapers, baby formula, children's clothing, toothbrushes, soap, and more, including plenty of cuddly stuffed animals to make a child feel more comfortable.

Buttermilk Pancakes with Strawberry Topping

Pancakes
3/4 cup all-purpose flour
2 to 3 tablespoons sugar
1/2 teaspoon baking powder
1/2 teaspoon baking soda
1 teaspoon salt
1 egg
2 tablespoons corn oil
1 cup (or more) buttermilk

Strawberry Topping
orange juice
vanilla yogurt
sliced fresh strawberries
confectioners' sugar

For the pancakes, mix the flour, sugar, baking powder, baking soda and salt in a bowl. Add the egg, corn oil and enough buttermilk to make the desired consistency, mixing until smooth.

Drop by spoonfuls onto a generously buttered griddle or skillet. Bake until golden brown on both sides, turning once. Stack 2 or 3 pancakes on each serving plate.

For the topping, drizzle orange juice over the stacks and spread with yogurt. Top with fresh strawberries and sprinkle with confectioners' sugar. Serve with white corn syrup.

You can double the recipe if needed or prepare the batter the night before and store in the refrigerator.

Serves 3 to 4

Breakfast Pizza

1 pound Honeysuckle White®
    Turkey Sausage
1 (8-ounce) can refrigerator crescent
    dinner rolls
1 cup frozen hash brown potatoes, thawed
1 cup (4 ounces) shredded
    Cheddar cheese

5 medium eggs, beaten
1/4 cup milk
1/2 teaspoon salt
1/4 teaspoon pepper
1/4 cup (1 ounce) grated
    Parmesan cheese

Preheat the oven to 375 degrees. Squeeze the sausage from the casings into a medium skillet. Cook over medium heat for 6 to 10 minutes or until no longer pink; drain.

Unroll the crescent roll dough and separate into rolls. Arrange the rolls in a round 12-inch pizza pan with the points toward the center. Press over the bottom and up the side of the pan to form the crust, sealing the perforations. Sprinkle with the cooked sausage, potatoes and Cheddar cheese. Combine the eggs, milk, salt and pepper in a medium bowl. Pour slowly over the pizza and top with the Parmesan cheese. Bake for 25 minutes or until the crust is golden brown and the topping is heated through. Slice into 8 wedges to serve.

Serves 8

Sausage Bundles

1 pound bulk pork sausage, crumbled
8 ounces cream cheese, softened
1 (4-ounce) can chopped green chiles

3 (8-count) cans refrigerator
    crescent rolls

Preheat the oven to 350 degrees. Brown the sausage in a skillet, stirring until crumbly; drain. Add the cream cheese and undrained green chiles. Cook over medium heat until the cream cheese melts, stirring to mix well.

Separate each can of crescent rolls into 4 rectangles, pressing the perforations between triangles to seal. Cut each rectangle into 2 squares. Press the squares into miniature muffin cups. Spoon 2 tablespoons of the sausage mixture into each cup. Pull up the corners to enclose the filling and twist lightly. Bake for 25 to 30 minutes or until golden brown.

Serves 12

Baked Eggs Benedict

12 slices Canadian bacon
12 slices Swiss cheese
12 eggs

1 cup heavy cream
1/3 cup grated Parmesan cheese
paprika and pepper to taste

Preheat the oven to 450 degrees. Arrange the Canadian bacon in a 9×12-inch baking pan sprayed with nonstick cooking spray. Top each bacon slice with a slice of Swiss cheese. Break 1 egg carefully over each slice of cheese, taking care not to break the yolks. Pour the cream gently over the eggs.

Bake for 10 minutes. Reduce the oven temperature to 350 degrees. Sprinkle the eggs with the Parmesan cheese, paprika and pepper. Bake for 10 minutes longer or until set.

Serves 12

Brunch Casserole

1 pound bulk pork sausage, crumbled
7 eggs
2 cups milk
1 1/2 to 2 tablespoons
    Worcestershire sauce
2 cups torn or chopped spinach
1 large tomato, coarsely chopped

3 cups (12 ounces) shredded sharp
    Cheddar cheese
1 teaspoon dry mustard
salt and pepper to taste
8 slices bread, crusts trimmed
    and cubed

Brown the sausage in a skillet, stirring until crumbly; drain. Combine the eggs, milk, Worcestershire sauce, spinach, tomato, cheese, dry mustard, salt and pepper in a bowl; mix well. Fold in the sausage and bread cubes.

Spoon the mixture into a 9×13-inch baking dish. Chill for 5 hours or longer.

Preheat the oven to 325 degrees. Bake the casserole for 1 hour or until set and the cheese is bubbly. You can also bake the mixture in greased miniature muffin cups for 10 to 12 minutes or in large muffin cups for 25 to 30 minutes.

Serves 8

Green Chile Eggs

2 (4-ounce) cans whole
  green chiles
3 cups (12 ounces) shredded Monterey
  Jack cheese

3 cups (12 ounces) shredded
  Cheddar cheese
2 (5-ounce) cans evaporated milk
6 eggs, lightly beaten

Preheat the oven to 350 degrees. Rinse and cut open the green chiles, discarding the seeds. Arrange in a 8×10-inch baking dish and sprinkle with the Monterey Jack cheese and Cheddar cheese.

Combine the evaporated milk and eggs in a bowl and mix well. Pour over the layers. Bake for 40 minutes. Cool for 10 minutes before serving. You can prepare this the night before and chill until baking time.

Serves 8 to 10

Spanish Eggs

7 slices bacon
1 onion, finely chopped
1/2 green bell pepper, thinly sliced
1 (10-ounce) can tomatoes with
  green chiles, drained

2 (4-ounce) cans sliced mushrooms
9 eggs, beaten
butter
1 cup (4 ounces) shredded cheese

Preheat the broiler. Cook the bacon in a skillet until crisp; remove to a paper towel to drain. Add the onion and bell pepper to the skillet and sauté until the onion is translucent. Add the drained tomatoes with green chiles and mushrooms. Cook until thickened, stirring frequently.

Cook the eggs in a small amount of butter in a skillet, stirring until soft set. Remove to an ovenproof serving platter and top with the tomato mixture, shredded cheese and crumbled bacon. Broil just until the cheese melts.

Serves 6

Mushroom Empanadas

Cream Cheese Pastry
1/2 cup (1 stick) butter, softened
9 ounces cream cheese, softened
1 1/2 cups all-purpose flour
1/2 teaspoon salt

Empanadas
1 large onion, minced
8 ounces fresh mushrooms, chopped
3 tablespoons butter
1/4 teaspoon thyme
1/2 teaspoon salt
1/2 teaspoon pepper
2 tablespoons all-purpose flour
1/4 cup sour cream
1 egg
1 teaspoon milk

For the pastry, cream the butter and cream cheese in a mixing bowl until light and fluffy. Add the flour and salt and mix to form a dough. Roll 1/8 inch thick on a floured surface and cut into 3-inch circles.

For the empanadas, preheat the oven to 450 degrees. Sauté the onion and mushrooms in the melted butter in a large skillet for 3 minutes. Add the thyme, salt and pepper. Sprinkle with the flour and mix well. Stir in the sour cream and cook until thickened, stirring frequently.

Place 1 spoonful of the mushroom mixture in the center of each pastry round and fold over to enclose the filling; press the edges to seal. Place on an ungreased baking sheet.

Beat the egg and milk lightly in a small bowl; brush on the pastries. Bake for 10 to 15 minutes or until golden brown or freeze to bake later.

Makes 36

Rosemary Cookies

Don't forget…

Desserts

Don't think of dessert as the end of the meal.

It's the topping, the icing—it's what seals the deal.

A trifle, a truffle, a cake or two,

And only the tastiest cookie will do.

This chapter graciously underwritten by Masterfoods, USA

Mocha Velvet Torte

Raspberry Coulis
2 (10-ounce) packages frozen
   raspberries, thawed
1/4 cup sugar
3 tablespoons Grand Marnier

Torte
1 tablespoon instant coffee granules
1 cup boiling water
1 1/2 cups sugar
2 1/2 cups (15 ounces) semisweet
   chocolate chips

1 1/2 cups (3 sticks) butter, melted
6 eggs
1 teaspoon vanilla extract

Chocolate Ganache
8 ounces bittersweet chocolate,
   chopped
1 cup heavy cream
1 1/2 tablespoons butter

Garnish: fresh raspberries

For the coulis, process the raspberries in a food processor until puréed. Strain into a bowl and stir in the sugar and liqueur. Store in the refrigerator for up to 1 week.

For the torte, preheat the oven to 225 degrees. Line a greased 9-inch springform pan with waxed paper and grease the waxed paper. Dissolve the coffee granules in the boiling water in a bowl. Add the sugar, stirring to dissolve completely. Process the chocolate chips in a food processor for 1 1/2 minutes until finely chopped, stopping once to scrape down the side. Add the coffee mixture through the tube, processing to mix well and stopping once to scrape down the side. Add the butter and then the eggs 1 at a time, pulsing to mix well after each addition. Add the vanilla and pulse once. Spoon into the prepared springform pan. Bake for 2 1/2 hours or just until firm to the touch. Cool on a wire rack. Loosen from the side of the pan with a knife and invert onto an 8-inch cardboard round. Place on a rack over a shallow pan.

For the ganache, simmer 2/3 of the chocolate and the cream in a double boiler over water, stirring until blended well. Add 1/3 of the butter and continue to heat, stirring to blend. Add the remaining chocolate and stir until smooth. Stir in the remaining butter.

To assemble and serve, cool the ganache until slightly thickened but still of pouring consistency. Pour over the torte, covering completely. Chill in the refrigerator for 8 hours. Cut into wedges. Spoon the raspberry coulis onto serving plates and place a wedge of the torte on each plate. Garnish with fresh raspberries.

Serves 10

Crème Brûlée

2 cups heavy cream
6 egg yolks
$^{1}/_{2}$ cup granulated sugar
1 tablespoon brown sugar

$^{1}/_{2}$ teaspoon vanilla extract
$^{1}/_{4}$ cup granulated sugar

Garnish: *fresh berries*

Preheat the oven to 300 degrees. Heat the cream in a heavy saucepan over medium heat until steam begins to rise. Remove from the heat, cover, and let stand for 15 minutes. Beat the egg yolks with $^{1}/_{2}$ cup granulated sugar and the brown sugar in a mixing bowl until well mixed. Add the cream and vanilla gradually, beating constantly.

Spoon the mixture into four 6-ounce ramekins and place in a baking pan. Add hot water to within $^{1}/_{2}$ inch of the tops of the ramekins. Bake for 25 to 30 minutes or just until the centers of the custard are set. Cool on a wire rack. Cover with plastic wrap and chill in the refrigerator. Sprinkle $^{1}/_{4}$ cup granulated sugar over the tops of the custards. Broil or heat with a kitchen torch until the sugar bubbles and caramelizes to a medium brown. Garnish with berries, if desired. You can also serve the custards without topping.

Serves 4

Pots de Crème

1 cup (6 ounces) chocolate chips
2 tablespoons sugar
1 egg
1 tablespoon rum or coffee (optional)
1 teaspoon vanilla extract

salt to taste
$^{3}/_{4}$ cup milk

Garnish: *whipped cream*

Combine the chocolate chips, sugar, egg, rum, vanilla and salt in a blender and blend until smooth. Bring the milk just to a boil in a heavy saucepan. Add to the blender and process for 1 minute or until smooth. Spoon into ramekins and chill until set. Garnish with whipped cream.

If raw eggs are a problem in your area, use an equivalent amount of pasteurized egg substitute.

Serves 4

Dutch Apple Crisp

 1 (20-ounce) can sliced apples or
    apple pie filling
1 cup all-purpose flour, sifted
3/4 cup packed brown sugar

1 teaspoon cinnamon
1/2 teaspoon nutmeg
1/4 teaspoon salt
1/2 cup (1 stick) butter, sliced

Preheat the oven to 350 degrees. Spread the apples in a greased shallow 1½-quart baking dish. Combine the flour, brown sugar, cinnamon, nutmeg and salt in a bowl and mix well. Cut in the butter until crumbly. Sprinkle on the apples.

Bake for 40 minutes or until the topping is slightly crusty and golden brown. Serve warm with a scoop of vanilla ice cream.

Serves 6

Peach Cobbler

1 quart sliced fresh or frozen peaches
1 cup water
1 cup sugar
1 tablespoon lemon juice
6 tablespoons (3/4 stick) butter
1 cup baking mix

1/2 cup sugar
salt to taste
1 tablespoon wheat germ
2 tablespoons butter
cinnamon and nutmeg to taste

Preheat the oven to 350 degrees. Combine the peaches, water, 1 cup sugar and the lemon juice in a medium saucepan and bring to a boil.

Melt 6 tablespoons butter in a saucepan and stir in the baking mix, 1/2 cup sugar and salt. Reserve 1/2 cup of the mixture. Spread the remaining mixture in an 8×8-inch or 2-quart baking pan and top with the peaches.

Mix the wheat germ with the reserved baking mix mixture and sprinkle over the fruit. Dot with 2 tablespoons butter and sprinkle with cinnamon and nutmeg. Bake for 40 to 45 minutes or until golden brown and bubbly. You can also use this recipe to make a blackberry or dewberry cobbler.

Serves 4 to 6

Crème de Menthe Parfaits

1 quart vanilla ice cream, softened
1 pint lime sherbet, softened
4^1/2 ounces whipped topping
^{1}/4 cup green crème de menthe
1 cup whipping cream

^{1}/2 cup confectioners' sugar
^{1}/2 teaspoon vanilla extract

Garnish: *mint or chocolate curls*

Process the ice cream, sherbet, whipped topping and crème de menthe in a blender until smooth. Spoon into 6 parfait glasses and freeze for 3 to 4 hours or until firm.

Let stand at room temperature for several minutes to soften. Whip the whipping cream with the confectioners' sugar and vanilla in a bowl until soft peaks form. Spoon on the tops of the parfaits and garnish with mint or chocolate curls.

Serves 6

Caramel Dumplings

Caramel Sauce
2 cups sugar
2 tablespoons butter
2 cups boiling water
1 teaspoon vanilla extract
salt to taste

Dumplings
^{1}/2 cup milk
1 cup all-purpose flour
^{1}/2 cup sugar
2 tablespoons baking powder
2 tablespoons (rounded) butter, softened

For the sauce, sprinkle ^{1}/2 cup of the sugar in a skillet. Cook until the sugar caramelizes to a medium brown. Add the remaining 1^1/2 cups sugar, butter, boiling water, vanilla and salt, stirring to mix well; lumps may form, but will dissolve as the sauce cooks. Boil for 4 minutes. Spoon into a baking dish.

For the dumplings, preheat the oven to 350 degrees. Combine the milk, flour, sugar, baking powder and butter in a bowl and mix to form a dough. Drop by spoonfuls into the sauce in the baking dish; dumplings may appear to run together.

Bake for 25 minutes. Cool slightly and serve warm with ice cream or whipped cream.

Serves 6

Milky Way Ice Cream

6 cups milk
7 (4-inch) Milky Way® candy bars
36 large marshmallows
1¹/₂ quarts heavy cream

Heat the milk in a double boiler. Add the candy bars and marshmallows and cook until melted, stirring to blend well. Remove from the heat and cool to room temperature.

Add the cream and mix well. Pour into a 6-quart ice cream freezer and freeze using the manufacturer's instructions.

Serves 8 to 10

Chocolate Mint Ice Cream

1¹/₂ cups sugar
6 cups milk
2 quarts heavy cream
2 (14-ounce) cans sweetened condensed milk
4 teaspoons peppermint extract
8 ounces dark chocolate
green food coloring

Garnish: *fresh mint and/or edible flowers*

Combine the sugar, milk, cream, sweetened condensed milk and peppermint extract in an ice cream freezer container. Freeze for 20 to 30 minutes or until partially frozen, using the manufacturer's instructions.

Melt the chocolate in a double boiler. Drizzle into the ice cream freezer container and add the desired amount of food coloring. Freeze until of the desired consistency. Garnish servings with mint or edible flowers.

Serves 16 to 20

Chocolate Toffee Ice Cream Bar Dessert

Fudge Sauce
2 cups confectioners' sugar
1¹/₂ cups evaporated milk
²/₃ cup (4 ounces) chocolate chips
¹/₂ cup (1 stick) butter
1 teaspoon vanilla extract

Dessert
1 (16-ounce) package cream-filled
    chocolate sandwich cookies, crushed
¹/₂ cup (1 stick) butter, melted
1¹/₂ cups toffee bits
¹/₂ gallon vanilla ice cream, softened

For the sauce, combine the confectioners' sugar, evaporated milk, chocolate chips and butter in a saucepan. Bring to a boil and cook for 8 minutes, stirring constantly. Remove from the heat and stir in the vanilla. Cool completely.

For the dessert, mix the cookie crumbs with the butter in a bowl. Press in a greased 9×13-inch dish and sprinkle with the toffee bits. Spread the ice cream over the chips and freeze for 2 to 3 hours or until firm.

Spread the sauce over the ice cream layer and freeze until serving time.

Serves 8 to 12

Heritage Square

In 1999, the Junior League gave $40,000 to the Keep Waco Beautiful organization to fund the "Walkway of Community Service" at Heritage Square, the City of Waco's new memorial park in the heart of downtown Waco. Set in front of Waco City Hall, Heritage Square is a lovely tribute to the people and organizations that have together made Waco a wonderful place to live. Included in the "Walkway of Community Service" are all of the Junior League of Waco's past presidents and community projects.

Bread Pudding

4 cups sugar
1 tablespoon cinnamon
1/8 teaspoon nutmeg
6 eggs
1 quart (or more) heavy cream

1 tablespoon vanilla extract
2 to 3 loaves French bread or
    panettone, cubed
1 cup raisins
Whiskey Sauce (below)

Preheat the oven to 325 degrees. Mix the sugar, cinnamon and nutmeg in a large bowl. Add the eggs and whisk until smooth. Add the cream and vanilla and mix well. Fold in the bread and raisins. Adjust the consistency with more bread or cream if necessary.

Spoon into a buttered 9×13-inch baking pan. Bake for 50 minutes or until the top is golden brown and a wooden pick inserted into the center comes out clean. Serve warm with Whiskey Sauce.

You can soak the raisins in bourbon for added flavor, if desired.

Serves 12

Whiskey Sauce

2 tablespoons cornstarch
1/4 cup water
4 cups (1 quart) heavy cream

1 cup sugar, or to taste
1/2 cup bourbon, or to taste

Whisk the cornstarch into the water in a bowl. Bring the cream to a boil in a saucepan and add the cornstarch mixture, whisking vigorously. Return to a boil and cook until thickened, whisking constantly. Remove from the heat. Whisk in the sugar and bourbon gradually, testing several times for the desired taste.

Serves 12

Butterscotch Cake

1 (2-layer) package yellow cake mix
1 (4-ounce) package vanilla instant
  pudding mix
1 (4-ounce) package butterscotch instant
  pudding mix
3/4 cup water
4 eggs
1 cup (6 ounces) butterscotch chips
1/2 cup packed brown sugar
1/2 cup chopped nuts

Preheat the oven to 350 degrees. Combine the cake mix, vanilla pudding mix, butterscotch pudding mix, water and eggs in a mixing bowl and beat for 4 minutes. Mix the butterscotch chips, brown sugar and nuts in a small bowl.

Layer the cake batter and the chips mixture 1/3 at a time in a greased 10-inch tube pan. Bake for 1 hour and 20 minutes. Cool the cake in the pan on a wire rack for 20 minutes, then invert onto a cake plate to cool completely.

Serves 12

School Supply Train

Pens, pencils, notebooks, and backpacks: they're things that most kids take for granted when getting ready to start the school year. Sadly, many local students don't show up on the first day of school with the proper supplies. The School Supply Train was organized to provide brand new school supplies to kids whose families could not afford them. Junior League members collected supplies, assembled packages, and distributed them to 2,000 elementary school children each year since 1996. In 2001, the League successfully transitioned the program to the Salvation Army.

Carrot Cake

1 (2-layer) package yellow cake mix
1 (3¹/₂-ounce) package vanilla instant
    pudding mix
²/₃ cup fresh orange juice
¹/₂ cup vegetable oil
4 eggs
2 teaspoons cinnamon
3 cups grated carrots,
    about 5 medium carrots
¹/₂ cup raisins
1 (8-ounce) can crushed pineapple,
    drained
1 (3¹/₂-ounce) can flaked coconut
¹/₂ cup chopped walnuts or pecans
Cream Cheese Frosting (page 157)

Preheat the oven to 350 degrees. Combine the cake mix, pudding mix, orange juice, vegetable oil, eggs and cinnamon in a large mixing bowl. Beat at low speed for 1 minute and scrape down the side of the bowl. Beat at medium speed for 2 minutes longer. Scrape down the side of the bowl. Fold in the carrots, raisins, pineapple, coconut and walnuts.

Spoon the batter into 2 greased and floured 9-inch cake pans. Bake for 30 to 35 minutes or until a wooden pick inserted into the center comes out clean. Cool in the pans on a wire rack for 10 minutes. Loosen the layers from the pans by running a knife around the edge. Invert the layers onto a wire rack to cool completely. Spread Cream Cheese Frosting between the layers and over the top and side of the cake. Chill for 20 minutes for the frosting to set before serving.

Serves 18

Mexican Pineapple Cake

2 cups all-purpose flour
2 cups sugar
2 teaspoons baking soda
2 eggs, lightly beaten
1 (20-ounce) can crushed pineapple
1 cup chopped roasted pecans
Cream Cheese Frosting (below)
chopped pecans

Preheat the oven to 350 degrees. Combine the flour, sugar, baking soda, eggs and undrained pineapple in a mixing bowl and mix until smooth. Stir in 1 cup pecans. Spoon into a greased and floured 9×13-inch cake pan and bake for 40 to 45 minutes or until the cake tests done.

Spread the Cream Cheese Frosting over the hot cake. Sprinkle with additional chopped pecans and cool on a wire rack.

Serves 12

Cream Cheese Frosting

8 ounces cream cheese, softened
1/2 cup (1 stick) margarine, melted
1 (16-ounce) package confectioners' sugar
1 teaspoon vanilla extract

Combine the cream cheese, margarine, confectioners' sugar and vanilla in a mixing bowl and beat until light and fluffy.

Serves 12

Rum Cake

Cake
1/2 cup chopped pecans
1 (2-layer) package yellow cake mix
1 (3 1/2-ounce) package vanilla
    instant pudding mix
4 eggs
1/2 cup water
1/2 cup vegetable oil
1/2 cup rum

Rum Glaze
1/2 cup rum
1 cup sugar
1/2 cup (1 stick) butter
1/4 cup water

For the cake, preheat the oven to 325 degrees. Oil a bundt pan and sprinkle with sugar. Spread the pecans in the prepared pan. Combine the cake mix, pudding mix, eggs, water, vegetable oil and rum in a mixing bowl and beat at high speed for 4 minutes.

Spoon the batter over the pecans in the bundt pan. Bake for 60 to 70 minutes or until the cake tests done. Cool in the pan on a wire rack for 20 minutes.

For the glaze, combine the rum, sugar, butter and water in a medium saucepan. Bring to a boil and cook for 3 minutes, stirring constantly to blend well.

Pour the glaze over the cake in the bundt pan. Let stand on the wire rack until completely cool. Invert onto a cake plate.

Serves 12

Turtle Cake

Cake
1 (2-layer) package German's chocolate cake mix
¹/₂ cup (1 stick) butter or margarine, softened
1¹/₂ cups water
¹/₂ cup vegetable oil
¹/₂ (14-ounce) can sweetened
    condensed milk

Caramel Filling
1 (16-ounce) package caramels, unwrapped
¹/₂ (14-ounce) can sweetened condensed milk
¹/₂ to 1 cup chopped pecans

Chocolate Frosting
¹/₂ cup (1 stick) butter
3 tablespoons baking cocoa
6 tablespoons evaporated milk
1 (16-ounce) package confectioners' sugar
1 teaspoon vanilla extract

For the cake, preheat the oven to 350 degrees. Combine the cake mix, butter, water, vegetable oil and sweetened condensed milk in a mixing bowl and mix until smooth. Spread half the batter in a greased and floured 9×13-inch cake pan. Bake for 20 to 25 minutes.

For the filling, melt the caramels with the sweetened condensed milk in a saucepan, stirring to blend evenly. Spread evenly over the baked cake layer and sprinkle with the pecans. Spread the remaining cake batter over the caramel layer and bake for 20 to 25 minutes longer or until the cake tests done.

For the frosting, combine the butter, baking cocoa and evaporated milk in a saucepan and cook until the butter melts, stirring to blend well. Stir in the confectioners' sugar and vanilla. Spread over the cake.

You can substitute a jar of marshmallow creme for the caramel filling and add a cup of chopped pecans to the batter, if desired.

Serves 24

Chocolate Krispies

1/2 cup (1 stick) butter
2 cups peanut butter
1 (16-ounce) package confectioners' sugar
3 1/2 cups crisp rice cereal
1 1/2 cups chopped pecans
1 (8-ounce) chocolate candy bar
1 cup (6 ounces) chocolate chips
1/2 bar paraffin

Melt the butter in a saucepan. Add the peanut butter, confectioners' sugar, cereal and pecans; mix well. Shape into balls.

Melt the chocolate bar and chocolate chips with the paraffin in a double boiler, stirring to blend well. Dip the cereal balls into the chocolate, coating evenly. Place on waxed paper to cool. You can freeze these, if desired.

Makes 4 dozen

Chocolate Truffles

1 (16-ounce) package cream-filled chocolate
  sandwich cookies, crushed
8 ounces cream cheese, softened
24 ounces semisweet chocolate

Combine the cookie crumbs and cream cheese in a mixing bowl and beat until well mixed. Shape by teaspoonfuls into balls.

Melt the chocolate in a double boiler. Dip the balls into the chocolate, coating evenly. Place on a waxed paper-lined tray. Chill for 2 hours or until the chocolate is set. Store in an airtight container in the refrigerator.

Makes 3 dozen

Mexican Fudge

1 (16-ounce) package confectioners' sugar
1 egg, lightly beaten
1/4 cup sweetened condensed milk
1/2 cup (1 stick) butter
4 (1-ounce) squares unsweetened baking chocolate
2 tablespoons instant coffee granules
2 teaspoons cinnamon
1 teaspoon vanilla extract
1 cup chopped nuts (optional)

Sift the confectioners' sugar into a large bowl. Add the egg and sweetened condensed milk and mix well with a rubber spatula. Combine the butter and chocolate in a double boiler and heat over simmering water until melted. Add the instant coffee granules and cinnamon and mix well.

Add the chocolate mixture to the confectioners' sugar mixture and mix until smooth. Stir in the vanilla and nuts. Spoon into a buttered 8×8-inch dish. Chill for 2 hours or longer. Cut into small squares to serve.

Makes 3 dozen

Safety Comes First

Safety 1st was a two-part project created in 1999 to address safety issues from infancy through the teenage years. A collaboration with the Safe Kids Coalition provided for car seat checks by certified safety technicians, as well as for bicycle safety seminars. The Neon Drunk Driving Simulator offered high school students a chance to see how alcohol and drugs impair a person's ability to drive.

Millionaire Candy

50 caramels, unwrapped
2 tablespoons margarine
2 tablespoons water

3 cups chopped pecans
1/3 block paraffin
2 cups (12 ounces) chocolate chips

Combine the caramels, margarine and water in a heavy saucepan and cook until the caramels and margarine melt, stirring to mix well. Stir in the pecans. Drop by spoonfuls onto a waxed paper-lined tray. Chill for 1 or 2 hours.

Melt the paraffin in a double boiler over low heat. Add the chocolate chips and heat until the chocolate melts, stirring to blend evenly. Dip the candy into the chocolate mixture, coating well. Place on waxed paper to cool.

Makes 3 dozen

Fabuloso Pralines

2 cups sugar
1 cup buttermilk
1 teaspoon baking soda
1/4 teaspoon salt

2 tablespoons butter
1/2 cup pecan halves
1 teaspoon vanilla extract

Combine the sugar, buttermilk, baking soda and salt in a large skillet. Cook over medium heat until the mixture reaches the soft-ball stage, stirring occasionally. Remove from the heat and stir in the butter. Add the pecans and then the vanilla.

Beat the mixture until slightly thickened. Drop onto waxed paper and let stand until cool and firm.

Makes 3 dozen

Brazos Brownies

Brownies
8 (1-ounce) squares unsweetened
 baking chocolate
1 cup (2 sticks) butter
5 eggs
3 cups sugar
1 tablespoon vanilla extract
1$^1/_2$ cups all-purpose flour

Brownie Frosting
$^1/_4$ cup baking cocoa
$^1/_2$ cup (1 stick) butter
$^1/_3$ cup milk
1 (16-ounce) package confectioners' sugar

For the brownies, preheat the oven to 375 degrees. Melt the chocolate with the butter in a double boiler or heavy saucepan, stirring to blend well. Let stand until cool.

Combine the eggs, sugar and vanilla in a mixing bowl and beat at high speed for 10 minutes. Blend in the chocolate mixture. Fold in the flour, mixing just until combined. Spoon into a greased 9×13-inch baking pan. Bake for 35 minutes.

For the frosting, combine the baking cocoa, butter and milk in a saucepan. Cook until the butter melts and the mixture is bubbly, stirring constantly. Pour over the confectioners' sugar in a mixing bowl and mix until smooth.

Spread the frosting over the warm brownies and let stand until cool before cutting.

Makes 2 dozen

Chocolate Oatmeal Carmelitas

2 cups all-purpose flour
2 cups rolled oats
1¹/₂ cups packed brown sugar
1 teaspoon baking soda
¹/₂ teaspoon salt
1¹/₂ cups (3 sticks) margarine, melted
2 cups (12 ounces) chocolate chips
1 cup nuts
1¹/₂ cups caramel ice cream topping
6 tablespoons all-purpose flour

Preheat the oven to 350 degrees. Combine the flour, oats, brown sugar, baking soda, salt and margarine in a bowl and mix well. Press half the mixture in a 9×13-inch baking pan. Bake for 10 minutes. Sprinkle the chocolate chips and nuts over the top.

Combine the ice cream topping and flour in a bowl and mix until smooth. Drizzle over the chocolate chips and nuts. Sprinkle the remaining oats mixture over the topping. Bake for 15 to 20 minutes longer or until golden brown. Cool on a wire rack. Chill in the refrigerator before cutting to serve.

Makes 2 dozen

Peanut Butter Oatmeal Cookies with Chocolate Chips

1/2 cup (1 stick) butter, softened
1 1/2 cups sugar
1 1/2 cups packed brown sugar
4 eggs
1 teaspoon vanilla extract
2 cups chunky peanut butter

2 1/2 teaspoons baking soda
3 cups quick-cooking oats
3 cups rolled oats
1 cup (6 ounces) chocolate chips
1 cup (6 ounces) miniature "M&M's"
    Chocolate Candies®

Preheat the oven to 350 degrees. Combine the butter, sugar, brown sugar, eggs and vanilla in a mixing bowl and beat until smooth. Add the peanut butter and mix well. Mix in the baking soda.

Stir in the oats, chocolate chips and "M&M's". Drop by spoonfuls onto an ungreased cookie sheet. Bake for 6 minutes or just until light brown; do not overcook. Cool on the cookie sheet for 5 minutes, then remove to a wire rack to cool completely.

Makes 5 dozen

CAPP

Every child has a right to be safe, strong, and free: that's the cornerstone of the Child Assault Prevention Program (CAPP), a joint effort initiated in 2000 between the Junior League, Waco Independent School District, the Advocacy Center, and McLennan County Youth Collaboration. Through curriculum development, research and evaluation, public education, and training, CAPP teaches strategies for preventing verbal, physical, and sexual abuse. The program empowers children to recognize when someone is trying to take away their right to be safe, strong, and free.

Kahlúa Bars

Bars
1¹/₄ cups sifted all-purpose flour
³/₄ teaspoon baking powder
¹/₂ teaspoon salt
¹/₂ cup (1 stick) butter, softened
³/₄ cup packed brown sugar
1 egg
¹/₄ cup plus 2 tablespoons Kahlúa
¹/₃ cup chopped pecans or almonds
1 cup chopped Dove dark chocolate candy

Kahlúa Frosting
2 tablespoons butter
1 tablespoon Kahlúa
2 tablespoons milk or cream
1¹/₃ cups sifted confectioners' sugar

For the bars, preheat the oven to 350 degrees. Sift the flour with the baking powder and salt. Cream the butter and brown sugar in a mixing bowl until light and fluffy. Beat in the egg. Stir in ¹/₄ cup of the liqueur.

Add the flour mixture and mix well. Fold in the pecans and chocolate candy pieces. Spread in a greased 7×11-inch baking pan. Bake for 20 to 25 minutes or until the top springs back when lightly touched. Cool on a wire rack. Brush the top with the remaining liqueur.

For the frosting, melt the butter in a saucepan. Stir in the liqueur, milk and confectioners' sugar. Spread over the cooled baked layer. Cut into bars to serve.

Makes 3 dozen

White Chocolate Macadamia Cookies

2 cups all-purpose flour
1 teaspoon baking soda
1/2 teaspoon salt
1/2 cup (1 stick) butter, softened
1/2 cup shortening
1/2 cup granulated sugar
3/4 cup packed brown sugar
1 egg
1 1/2 teaspoons vanilla extract
6 ounces white baking chocolate,
    cut into small chunks
7 ounces macadamias, coarsely chopped

Preheat the oven to 350 degrees. Mix the flour, baking soda and salt together. Cream the butter and shortening at medium speed in a mixing bowl until light and fluffy. Add the granulated sugar and brown sugar gradually, beating constantly until fluffy. Beat in the egg and vanilla.

Add the flour mixture to the creamed mixture and mix well. Stir in the white chocolate chunks and macadamias. Drop by rounded spoonfuls 2 inches apart on cookie sheets lightly sprayed with nonstick cooking spray.

Bake the cookies for 8 to 10 minutes or until golden brown. Cool on the cookie sheets for several minutes, then remove to wire racks to cool completely.

Makes 3 dozen

Christmas Fruit Drop Cookies

3 1/2 cups all-purpose flour
1 teaspoon baking soda
1 teaspoon salt
1 cup shortening
2 cups packed brown sugar
2 eggs
1/2 cup milk
1/4 cup brandy
2 cups broken pecans
1 (16-ounce) container mixed candied fruit

Preheat the oven to 400 degrees. Sift the flour, baking soda and salt together. Cream the shortening and brown sugar in a mixing bowl until light and fluffy. Beat in the eggs, milk and brandy. Add the flour mixture gradually, mixing well. Stir in the pecans and candied fruit. Chill for 1 hour or longer.

Drop by teaspoonfuls 2 inches apart on greased cookie sheets. Bake for 8 to 10 minutes or until dark golden brown. Cool on the cookie sheets for several minutes, then remove to a wire rack to cool completely. Store in an airtight container indefinitely.

Makes 8 dozen

Jubilee Jumbles

Cookies
2 3/4 cups sifted all-purpose flour
1/2 teaspoon baking soda
1 teaspoon salt
1/2 cup shortening
1/2 cup granulated sugar
1 cup packed brown sugar
2 eggs
1 cup evaporated milk
1 teaspoon vanilla extract

Browned Butter Glaze
2 tablespoons butter
2 cups sifted confectioners' sugar
1/4 cup evaporated milk

For the cookies, preheat the oven to 350 degrees. Sift the flour, baking soda and salt together. Cream the shortening, granulated sugar and brown sugar in a mixing bowl until light and fluffy. Beat in the eggs. Stir in the evaporated milk and vanilla. Stir in the flour mixture. Chill in the refrigerator.

Drop by tablespoonfuls 2 inches apart on greased cookie sheets. Bake until golden brown.

For the glaze, cook the butter in a saucepan until golden brown. Add the confectioners' sugar and evaporated milk and mix well. Spread on the warm cookies. Decorate as desired.

You can also add 1 cup moist shredded coconut, finely chopped dates, seedless raisins, walnuts and/or chocolate chips to these cookies, if desired.

Makes 3 dozen

Rosemary Cookies

^{1}/2 cup (1 stick) butter, softened
^{1}/2 cup shortening
1^1/2 cups sugar
2 eggs
2^3/4 cups all-purpose flour

2 teaspoons cream of tartar
1 teaspoon baking soda
^{1}/4 teaspoon salt
2 teaspoons (scant) chopped
    fresh rosemary

Preheat the oven to 400 degrees. Cream the butter, shortening and sugar in a mixing bowl until light and fluffy. Beat in the eggs. Sift the flour into the mixture and mix well. Mix in the cream of tartar, baking soda, and salt. Add the rosemary and mix well.

Shape into small balls and place on a ungreased cookie sheet. Dip the bottom of a glass in additional sugar and press the cookies to flatten for a crunchy glaze. Bake for 8 minutes. Loosen from the cookie sheet immediately and remove to a wire rack to cool.

Makes 3 dozen

Layered Dessert Bars

^{1}/2 cup (1 stick) butter, melted
1 cup graham cracker crumbs
1 cup coconut
1 cup (6 ounces) chocolate chips

1 cup (6 ounces) toffee bits
^{1}/2 cup (3 ounces) butterscotch chips
1 cup sweetened condensed milk
1 cup chopped pecans

Preheat the oven to 300 degrees. Spread the butter in a 9×13-inch baking pan. Layer the graham cracker crumbs, coconut, chocolate chips, toffee bits and butterscotch chips in the pan in the order listed.

Drizzle with the sweetened condensed milk and sprinkle with the pecans. Bake for 30 minutes. Cool on a wire rack before cutting into bars.

Makes 2 dozen

Brownie Pie

1 unbaked (9-inch) deep-dish pie shell
1 cup (6 ounces) semisweet
   chocolate chips
1/4 cup (1/2 stick) butter or margarine
1/2 cup baking mix

1 (14-ounce) can sweetened
   condensed milk
2 eggs
1 teaspoon vanilla extract
1 cup chopped nuts (optional)

Preheat the oven to 375 degrees. Bake the pie shell for 10 minutes. Remove from the oven and reduce the oven temperature to 325 degrees.

Melt the chocolate chips with the butter in a saucepan over low heat, stirring to mix well. Beat with the next 4 ingredients in a mixing bowl until smooth. Stir in the nuts.

Spoon into the partially baked pie shell and bake for 35 to 40 minutes longer or until the center is set. Serve with vanilla ice cream or whipped cream.

Serves 8

Chocolate Pie

1/3 cup all-purpose flour
1 cup sugar
1 1/2 (1-ounce) squares unsweetened
   baking chocolate, grated
1 cup hot water
3 egg yolks

1 tablespoon margarine
1 teaspoon vanilla extract
1 cup hot water
1 baked (9-inch) pie shell
3 egg whites
sugar to taste

Preheat the oven to 350 degrees. Mix the flour and 1 cup sugar together. Combine the grated chocolate and 1 cup hot water in a double boiler and cook until the chocolate melts, stirring to blend well.

Add the flour mixture and egg yolks and mix well. Add the margarine, vanilla and 1 cup hot water; mix well. Cook until thickened, stirring constantly. Pour into the pie shell.

Beat the egg whites in a mixing bowl until frothy. Add the desired amount of sugar and beat until stiff peaks form. Spread over the pie, sealing to the edge. Bake for about 25 minutes or until golden brown.

Serves 8

Coconut Cream Pie

Pie
1 cup sugar
2 tablespoons all-purpose flour
3 tablespoons cornstarch
1/4 teaspoon (scant) salt
2 cups milk
3 egg yolks
1 tablespoon butter
1 teaspoon vanilla extract
1/4 teaspoon almond extract
1 (4-ounce) can minus 1/4 cup
    flaked coconut
1 baked (9-inch) pie shell

Coconut Meringue
3 egg whites
1/4 teaspoon cream of tartar
6 tablespoons sugar
1/2 teaspoon vanilla extract
1/4 teaspoon almond extract
1/4 cup flaked coconut reserved
    from the filling

For the filling, mix the sugar, flour, cornstarch and salt in a heavy saucepan. Stir in the milk gradually. Cook over medium heat until the mixture begins to boil and thicken, stirring constantly.

Beat the egg yolks in a bowl. Stir 3 or 4 tablespoons of the hot mixture into the egg yolks, then stir the egg yolks into the hot mixture. Cook for 3 to 4 minutes longer or until thickened, stirring constantly.

Remove from the heat and stir in the butter and flavorings. Reserve 1/4 cup of the coconut for the topping and stir the remaining coconut into the pie filling. Cool to room temperature and spoon into the pie shell.

For the meringue, preheat the oven to 325 degrees. Beat the egg whites with the cream of tartar in a small mixing bowl until soft peaks form. Add 3 tablespoons of the sugar, beating constantly. Add the remaining sugar and flavorings and beat until stiff peaks form.

Spread over the pie, sealing to the edge. Sprinkle with the reserved 1/4 cup coconut. Bake for 15 to 20 minutes or until golden brown.

Serves 8

Key Lime Pie

Graham Cracker Pie Shell
1¹/₂ cups graham cracker crumbs
6 tablespoons (³/₄ stick) butter, melted
¹/₂ cup sugar, or to taste
1 teaspoon cinnamon
¹/₂ teaspoon nutmeg

Filling
2 (14-ounce) cans sweetened
    condensed milk
4 egg yolks
³/₄ cup lime juice, about 12 to 14 limes

Garnish: *whipped cream*

For the pie shell, preheat the oven to 350 degrees. Mix the graham cracker crumbs, butter, sugar, cinnamon and nutmeg in a bowl. Press into a glass pie plate. Bake for 10 minutes. You can chill the pie shell for 10 minutes rather than baking it if preferred.

For the filling, combine the sweetened condensed milk, egg yolks and lime juice in a bowl and mix until thickened. Spoon into the pie shell. Bake for 8 to 10 minutes.

Cool completely on a wire rack. Chill, covered, in the refrigerator. Garnish with whipped cream and store in the refrigerator.

Serves 8 to 10

Showing Compassion

As its Millennium Gift to the community, the Junior League gave $250,000 to Compassion Ministries to construct a homeless shelter for women and children—the fastest-growing segment of homelessness in the area. Women living in the Hope House are able to achieve independent personal responsibility as they learn skills for positive employment, managing money, and establishing permanent housing for themselves. The Junior League continues to support Compassion Ministries by providing the children's program that is held during the parents' classes.

Mystery Pecan Pie

Pecan Pie Topping
1/4 cup sugar
1 cup light corn syrup
3 eggs, beaten
1 teaspoon vanilla extract

Pie
8 ounces cream cheese, softened
1/3 cup sugar
1 egg
1 teaspoon vanilla extract
1/4 teaspoon salt
1 unbaked (9-inch) deep-dish pie shell
1 to 1 1/2 cups chopped pecans

For the topping, combine the sugar, corn syrup, eggs and vanilla in a bowl and beat until smooth.

For the pie, preheat the oven to 375 degrees. Combine the cream cheese, sugar, egg, vanilla and salt in a bowl and beat until light and fluffy. Spread in the pie shell. Sprinkle with the pecans.

Spoon the topping over the pecans. Bake for 35 to 45 minutes or until the topping is firm to the touch. Cool on a wire rack.

Serves 8

A World of Color

In 2002, the Junior League brought Kaleidoscope to the children of our community. Created by Hallmark, Kaleidoscope is a magical place where kids can stretch their imaginations and explore their creative side through art. Kaleidoscope teaches problem-solving skills, positive self-esteem, practical and creative thinking, responsibility, and communication skills in an entertaining and exciting venue. The traveling exhibit was located in a cheerful purple pavilion in the parking lot of Richland Mall and welcomed 8,000 local school children to free fun.

Coconut Caramel Pecan Pie

6 tablespoons (3/4 stick) butter
1 cup flaked coconut
1 cup chopped pecans
8 ounces cream cheese,
    softened

1 (14-ounce) can sweetened
    condensed milk
16 ounces whipped topping
2 baked (9-inch) pie shells
1 (16-ounce) jar caramel sauce

Melt the butter in a medium skillet. Add the coconut and pecans and toast until light brown. Beat the cream cheese in a large mixing bowl until light and fluffy. Add the sweetened condensed milk and beat until smooth. Fold in the whipped topping.

Spread 1/4 of the cream cheese mixture in the pie shells. Layer the coconut/pecan mixture, the caramel sauce and the remaining cream cheese mixture 1/3 at a time in the pie shells. Chill until serving time.

Serves 16

Strawberry Pie

1 cup sugar
3 tablespoons cornstarch
1 cup water
several drops of red food coloring
3 tablespoons strawberry gelatin

1 pint strawberries, sliced
1 baked and cooled pie shell
1 cup whipping cream
1/4 cup sugar

Combine 1 cup sugar with the cornstarch, water and food coloring in a small saucepan and stir to mix well. Cook over medium heat until thickened to the consistency of pudding, stirring constantly. Remove from the heat and add the gelatin, stirring to dissolve completely. Fold in the strawberries. Spoon into the pie shell.

Beat the whipping cream in a mixing bowl until frothy. Add 1/4 cup sugar gradually, beating until soft peaks form. Spread on the pie. Store in the refrigerator.

Serves 8

Family-Friendly Fare

"No way—I don't like that!" is what you might hear

When finicky kids in your kitchen appear.

Try one of these fun, kid-friendly dishes.

Healthful and flavorful—just what everyone wishes.

This chapter graciously underwritten by Young Chefs Academy

Swiss Cheese Spread

4 cups (16 ounces) shredded
    Swiss cheese
1 bunch green onions, minced
1 cup mayonnaise

Combine the Swiss cheese, green onions and mayonnaise in a medium mixing bowl and mix well. Let stand until room temperature. Serve with crackers.

Makes 4 cups

Sweet Cream Dip

8 ounces cream cheese, softened
$^1/_3$ to $^1/_2$ cup granulated sugar, or to taste
$^1/_3$ to $^1/_2$ cup packed brown sugar, or to taste
8 ounces toffee bits, or to taste

Combine the cream cheese with the granulated sugar and brown sugar in a mixing bowl and beat until smooth. Stir in the toffee bits. Serve with sliced apples.

Serves 12

Great Discoveries

Where can children discover an entirely new country and culture without leaving Waco? In the People of the World Discovery Room located in the Harry and Anna Jeanes Discovery Center at the Mayborn Museum. The Junior League funded a gift of $107,464.73 for this room in Baylor University's world-class center of cultural and living history, natural science, and children's discovery which opened in May of 2004. The People of the World room truly offers a hands-on experience in world travel, from playing instruments and dancing to traditional music, to trying on clothes and exploring art and artifacts.

Cream Cheese Queso

1 pound hot bulk pork sausage
32 ounces cream cheese
2 (10-ounce) cans tomatoes with green chiles

Brown the sausage in a skillet, stirring until crumbly; drain. Add the cream cheese and undrained tomatoes with green chiles and cook until the cream cheese melts, stirring to mix well. Serve with corn chips.

Serves 12 to 15

Peppermint Hot Cocoa Mix

2 cups nonfat dry milk powder
³/4 cup sugar
¹/2 cup baking cocoa
¹/2 cup powdered nondairy creamer
¹/8 teaspoon salt
¹/2 cup miniature semisweet chocolate chips
¹/2 cup crushed peppermint candy

Combine the dry milk powder, sugar, baking cocoa, nondairy creamer and salt in a bowl and whisk to mix well. Stir in the chocolate chips and peppermint candy. Store in an airtight container at room temperature. Dissolve 3 tablespoons of the mixture in 6 ounces of boiling water in a cup to serve.

Makes 4 cups mix   —*From the kitchen of Young Chefs Academy*

Broccoli Soup

2 (10-ounce) packages frozen chopped broccoli, thawed
3 (10-ounce) cans cream of mushroom soup
3 soup cans water
2 (6-ounce) rolls jalapeño cheese, chopped

Garnish: croutons

Combine the broccoli, soup, water and cheese in a saucepan and mix well. Cook over low heat for 1 hour. Garnish servings with croutons.

Serves 6

Field Greens with Apple and Walnuts

Maple Balsamic Vinaigrette
2 tablespoons olive oil
2 tablespoons balsamic vinegar
1/4 cup maple syrup

Salad
6 ounces mixed field greens
1 medium green apple, sliced
3/4 cup crumbled blue cheese
1/2 cup glazed walnuts

For the vinaigrette, combine the olive oil, balsamic vinegar and maple syrup in a jar and shake to mix well.

For the salad, place the field greens in a salad bowl. Top with the apple slices, blue cheese and walnuts. Add the vinaigrette and toss to coat well.

Serves 4

Unforgettable Beef Tips

2 pounds stew beef
1 (10-ounce) can cream of mushroom soup
1 (10-ounce) can cream of celery soup
1 (10-ounce) can cream of chicken soup
1 (10-ounce) can French onion soup

Cut large pieces of stew beef into bite-size pieces. Combine with the mushroom soup, celery soup, chicken soup and French onion soup in a slow cooker sprayed with nonstick cooking spray and mix well.

Cook on Low for 8 hours or on High for 4 hours. Serve over cooked rice or noodles with a tossed salad and dessert.

Serves 6 to 8

Three-Packet Roast

1 (3¹/₂-pound) beef shoulder roast
1 envelope ranch salad dressing mix
1 envelope Italian salad dressing mix
1 envelope brown gravy mix
1 cup water
8 ounces fresh mushrooms, sliced

Place the roast in a slow cooker. Sprinkle with the ranch salad dressing mix, Italian salad dressing mix and gravy mix. Add the water. Cook on Low for 5 hours. Add the mushrooms and cook for 2 hours longer.

Serves 8

Teriyaki Flank Steak

2 tablespoons soy sauce
2 tablespoons dry sherry
1 tablespoon sugar
1 tablespoon honey
1 teaspoon unseasoned meat tenderizer
1 flank steak

Combine the soy sauce, wine, sugar, honey and meat tenderizer in a saucepan. Heat until the sugar dissolves, stirring to mix well. Combine with the flank steak in a sealable plastic bag. Marinate in the refrigerator for 3 to 4 hours.

Preheat the grill. Drain the steak and grill for 3 to 4 minutes on each side for medium rare or until done to taste. Serve with a green salad.

Serves 4

Stuffed Shells

2 pounds ground beef
3 garlic cloves, minced
1 tablespoon basil
1 tablespoon oregano
2 (16-ounce) jars spaghetti sauce
4 cups (16 ounces) shredded mozzarella cheese
12 ounces jumbo pasta shells, cooked and drained

Preheat the oven to 350 degrees. Brown the ground beef with the garlic, basil and oregano, stirring until the ground beef is crumbly; drain. Stir in 1/2 jar of the spaghetti sauce and half the cheese. Spoon the mixture into the cooked pasta shells.

Spread 1/2 jar of the spaghetti sauce in a 9×13-inch baking dish. Arrange the pasta shells seam side down in the prepared dish. Spoon the remaining spaghetti sauce over the shells and top with the remaining cheese. Bake for 30 to 40 minutes or until bubbly.

Serves 6 to 8

Stuffed Chicken

12 boneless skinless chicken breasts
1 jar sliced dried beef
12 slices bacon
2 cups (16 ounces) sour cream
2 (10-ounce) cans cream of mushroom soup

Pound the chicken to flatten. Place the dried beef slices on the chicken and roll to enclose the beef; wrap each with a slice of bacon and secure with a wooden pick. Arrange in a 9×13-inch baking dish.

Combine the sour cream and soup in a bowl and mix well. Spoon over the chicken. Chill for 8 hours or longer.

Preheat the oven to 275 degrees. Bake the chicken rolls, covered, for 1 hour. Bake, uncovered, for 2 hours longer. Remove the wooden picks before serving.

Serves 12

Sweet-and-Sour Chicken

12 chicken breasts
1 (8-ounce) bottle Russian salad dressing
1 envelope onion soup mix
1 (10-ounce) jar apricot preserves

Preheat the oven to 350 degrees. Arrange the chicken in a 9×13-inch baking dish. Combine the salad dressing, soup mix and preserves in a bowl and mix well. Spoon over the chicken. Bake for $1^{1}/2$ hours, basting occasionally. Serve hot with rice.

Serves 12

Green Chile Chicken Casserole

1¹/2 pounds chicken, cooked and chopped
1 (10-ounce) can mild green chile
  enchilada sauce
1 (4-ounce) can chopped green chiles

4 ounces light cream cheese
crushed tortilla chips
1 cup (4 ounces) shredded
  Monterey Jack cheese

Preheat the oven to 400 degrees. Combine the chicken with the enchilada sauce and green chiles in a saucepan. Simmer over medium heat for 5 minutes. Remove from the heat and add the cream cheese, stirring until the cream cheese melts.

Sprinkle a layer of tortilla chips in a greased 8×8-inch baking pan and spoon half the chicken mixture in the prepared pan. Repeat the layers and top with tortilla chips and the Monterey Jack cheese. Bake for 10 to 15 minutes or until bubbly.

Serves 4 to 6

Chicken Pot Pie

2 unbaked (9-inch) frozen pie pastries,
  thawed
2 cups chopped cooked chicken
2 (10-ounce) cans potato soup
1 (16-ounce) can mixed vegetables,
  drained

1/2 cup milk
1/2 teaspoon thyme
1/2 teaspoon pepper
1 egg, beaten (optional)

Preheat the oven to 375 degrees. Fit 1 of the pie pastries into a pie plate. Combine the chicken, soup, mixed vegetables, milk, thyme and pepper in a bowl and mix well. Spoon into the prepared pastry.

Fit the remaining pastry over the filling and press the edges to seal. Brush with the egg and bake for 40 minutes. Cool for 10 minutes before serving. Serve with fruit salad.

Serves 4 to 6

Spaghetti Pie

1 (8-ounce) package spaghetti
3 tablespoons margarine
1/4 cup (1 ounce) grated
    Parmesan cheese
1 egg

1/2 cup (4 ounces) sour cream
1 (32-ounce) jar spaghetti with
    meat sauce
2 cups (8 ounces) shredded
    mozzarella cheese

Preheat the oven to 350 degrees. Cook the spaghetti using the package directions; drain. Combine with the margarine and Parmesan cheese in a bowl; toss to coat well. Spread in a 9×13-inch baking dish. Combine the egg and sour cream in a small bowl and mix well. Spread over the spaghetti and top with the spaghetti sauce. Sprinkle the mozzarella cheese over the top. Bake for 30 minutes.

Serves 8

Spicy Sweet Potato Wedges

Spicy Sugar
1/4 cup packed brown sugar
1/4 teaspoon ginger
1/4 teaspoon salt
1/4 teaspoon cayenne pepper

Sweet Potato Wedges
4 or 5 large sweet potatoes
1/2 cup olive oil
1 teaspoon ground cumin
1 teaspoon ground coriander
1 teaspoon ground cloves

For the spicy sugar, mix the brown sugar, ginger, salt and cayenne pepper in a bowl.
For the sweet potatoes, preheat the oven to 425 degrees. Peel the sweet potatoes and cut into long thin wedges. Place in a large sealable bag. Add the olive oil, seal and rotate to coat evenly. Add the cumin, coriander and cloves; seal and rotate to coat well.

Spread the wedges in a single layer on a large baking sheet. Bake for 25 to 30 minutes or until tender. Serve immediately with the spicy sugar for dipping.

You can also serve the wedges with ketchup or a mixture of equal parts mayonnaise and Dijon mustard.

Serves 8

Baked Pineapple

3 eggs
1¹/₂ cups sugar
2 tablespoons (heaping)
    all-purpose flour

1 (20-ounce) can crushed pineapple
2 slices bread
¹/₂ cup (1 stick) butter, thinly sliced
brown sugar

Preheat the oven to 375 degrees. Beat the eggs in a mixing bowl. Add the sugar, flour and pineapple and mix well. Spoon into a greased 1¹/₂-quart baking dish.

Tear the bread into 1-inch cubes and sprinkle over the pineapple mixture. Top with the butter slices, covering the bread completely. Sprinkle with brown sugar.

Bake for 15 minutes or until heated through. Serve as a side dish or dessert.

Serves 6 to 8

Cheese Danish

2 large cans refrigerator crescent rolls
8 ounces cream cheese, softened
1 cup sugar
1 teaspoon vanilla extract

¹/₂ cup (1 stick) butter
¹/₂ cup sugar
¹/₂ teaspoon cinnamon

Preheat the oven to 350 degrees. Open 1 can of the crescent rolls and arrange the dough over the bottom and slightly up the sides of a greased 9×13-inch baking dish, pressing the perforations to seal.

Combine the cream cheese, 1 cup sugar and vanilla in a mixing bowl and mix until smooth. Spread in the prepared dish. Open the second can of crescent rolls and arrange over the filling, pressing the perforations and sides to seal.

Melt the butter in a saucepan and drizzle over the top. Mix ¹/₂ cup sugar and the cinnamon and sprinkle over the butter. Bake for 30 minutes or until golden brown. Cool for 10 minutes before serving.

Serves 12

Cheesy Toast

1 cup (4 ounces) shredded Cheddar cheese
*   or Swiss cheese*
¹/4 cup mayonnaise
¹/4 teaspoon garlic powder
¹/8 teaspoon white pepper
1 loaf French bread, sliced

Preheat the oven to 425 degrees. Combine the cheese, mayonnaise, garlic powder and white pepper in a medium mixing bowl and mix well. Spread on the bread slices. Arrange the bread slices on a baking sheet sprayed with nonstick cooking spray. Bake for 10 to 12 minutes or until slightly brown and bubbly.

Serves 12   *—From the kitchen of Young Chefs Academy*

Irish Soda Bread

2 cups all-purpose flour
2 tablespoons sugar
1 teaspoon baking powder
1 teaspoon baking soda
¹/2 teaspoon salt
3 tablespoons butter
1 cup buttermilk
¹/2 cup raisins (optional)

Preheat the oven to 350 degrees. Sift the flour, sugar, baking powder, baking soda and salt into a large bowl. Cut in the butter with 2 knives until crumbly. Stir in the buttermilk and raisins with a wooden spoon to make a dough.

Knead for 1 minute on a lightly floured surface. Shape and pat into a 6-inch circle; cut a cross ¹/2 inch deep in the top. Bake for 30 to 40 minutes or until golden brown. Rub the hot bread with additional butter.

Serves 8   *—From the kitchen of Young Chefs Academy*

PBJ Scones

3 cups all-purpose flour
1/2 cup sugar
2 teaspoons baking powder
1/2 teaspoon baking soda
1/2 teaspoon salt

3/4 cup (1 1/2 sticks) unsalted butter,
    chilled and cut into small pieces
1 cup low-fat buttermilk
2 tablespoons creamy peanut butter
1/4 cup jam

Preheat the oven to 425 degrees. Mix the flour, sugar, baking powder, baking soda and salt in a large bowl. Cut in the butter with a pastry cutter or 2 knives until the consistency of coarse cornmeal.

Add the buttermilk and mix with a fork. Mix in the peanut butter. Gather into a ball with the hands; do not overhandle the dough.

Shape and pat into a rectangle 1 inch thick on a lightly floured surface. Spread the jam on half the rectangle and fold the other half over the jam. Roll out into a long rectangle 3/4 inch thick.

Cut the dough into 12 squares and place 1/2 inch apart on an ungreased baking sheet. Bake for 14 to 15 minutes or until golden brown.

Serves 12

—From the kitchen of Young Chefs Academy

LEAPS

Lead, Empower And Promote Self-Esteem: that's what the Junior League chose as its newest project in 2004. Through extensive research and curriculum development, the League implemented a mentoring and reading program at North Waco Elementary, where League members are paired with one student for an entire school year. Building one-on-one relationships with students and their parents has had a positive effect on the students' behavior and reading skills, giving them the self-esteem to stay in school, study hard, and eventually to contribute their talents and skills for the good of their community.

Chocolate Chip Pound Cake

1 (2-layer) package yellow cake mix
1 (3½-ounce) package chocolate instant
    pudding mix
½ cup sugar
¾ cup vegetable oil
¾ cup water

4 eggs
1 cup (8 ounces) sour cream
½ cup (3 ounces) semisweet
    chocolate chips
confectioners' sugar or baking cocoa
    (optional)

Preheat the oven to 350 degrees. Combine the cake mix, pudding mix, sugar, vegetable oil, water, eggs and sour cream in a mixing bowl and beat until smooth. Stir in the chocolate chips.

Spoon into a greased bundt pan. Bake for 1 hour to 1¼ hours or until a wooden pick inserted into the center comes out clean. Cool on a wire rack and invert onto a serving plate. Dust with confectioners' sugar or baking cocoa.

Serves 12

German Chocolate Bundt Cake

1 (2-layer) package German chocolate
    cake mix
1 (16-ounce) can chocolate frosting
4 eggs, beaten

1 cup buttermilk
⅓ cup vegetable oil
2 cups (12 ounces) chocolate chips
confectioners' sugar

Preheat the oven to 325 degrees. Combine the cake mix, frosting, eggs, buttermilk and vegetable oil in a mixing bowl and mix until smooth. Stir in the chocolate chips.

Spoon into a greased bundt pan. Bake for 45 to 55 minutes or until the cake tests done. Cool on a wire rack. Invert onto a serving plate and dust with confectioners' sugar.

Serves 12

Pecan Bars

1 cup (2 sticks) butter
1 (16-ounce) package brown sugar
2 cups all-purpose flour
2 teaspoons baking powder
2 eggs
2 cups coarsely chopped pecans
vanilla extract to taste
1/2 teaspoon salt

Preheat the oven to 350 degrees. Place the butter in a 9×13-inch baking pan and place in the oven to melt. Add the brown sugar, flour, baking powder, eggs, pecans, vanilla and salt directly to the baking pan and stir to mix well.

Bake for 25 minutes. Cool slightly and cut into bars. Cover with a damp cloth.

Makes 2 dozen

Toffee Bars

1 (14-ounce) can sweetened condensed milk
2 rolls butter crackers, crushed
1 cup (6 ounces) toffee bits

Preheat the oven to 350 degrees. Place the sweetened condensed milk in a microwave-safe bowl. Microwave just until warm. Add the cracker crumbs and toffee bits and mix well.

Spread in a greased 9×9-inch baking pan. Bake for 20 minutes. Cool on a wire rack and cut into bars.

Makes 20

Apple Dew Dumplings

1 Granny Smith apple
1 (8-count) can refrigerator crescent rolls
1/2 cup (1 stick) butter, melted
3/4 cup sugar
1 teaspoon cinnamon
3/4 cup Mountain Dew

Preheat the oven to 350 degrees. Peel the apple and slice into 8 wedges. Unroll the crescent rolls and separate into triangles. Place 1 apple slice on each triangle and roll to enclose the apple. Place in a greased 8×8-inch baking pan.

Mix the butter, sugar and cinnamon in a small bowl. Sprinkle over the rolls. Add the Mountain Dew to the pan. Bake for 45 minutes. Serve warm with vanilla bean ice cream.

Serves 8

Baked Caramel Apples

4 apples, cored
2 tablespoons brown sugar
1/2 cup caramel ice cream topping
1/2 cup chopped pecans

Arrange the apples in a microwave-safe dish and sprinkle with brown sugar. Spoon 2 tablespoons of caramel topping over each apple and sprinkle with pecans. Microwave on High for 3 to 5 minutes or until the apples are tender.

Serves 4   *—From the kitchen of Young Chefs Academy*

Strawberries Romanoff

1 pint fresh strawberries, stemmed
$^1/_2$ cup (4 ounces) sour cream
3 tablespoons brown sugar
1 teaspoon brandy

Place the strawberries in a serving bowl. Combine the sour cream, brown sugar and brandy in a small bowl and mix well. Spoon over the strawberries. You can also serve the sour cream mixture as a dip.

Serves 4

Hot Fudge Sauce

1 cup sugar
2 tablespoons baking cocoa
$^1/_4$ cup ($^1/_2$ stick) margarine

$^1/_2$ cup half-and-half
1 teaspoon vanilla extract

Combine the sugar, baking cocoa, margarine, half-and-half and vanilla in a saucepan. Bring to a boil and boil for 4 minutes, stirring frequently. Let stand until thickened.

Serves 8

Granting Community Wishes

Every year, the Junior League sets aside a certain amount of money to meet critical needs in the community. Local nonprofit agencies can apply for critical needs funding in emergency situations, enabling them to continue their work in the community. Additionally, the League accepts applications for reactive funding from community agencies and organizations that need money to improve their services or fund special projects. The Talitha Koum Institute/Nurture Center, Waco Lions Park, and Waco-McLennan County Library are just a few of the agencies that have benefited from the League's reactive funding opportunities.

Oyster Crackers

1 envelope buttermilk salad dressing mix
1 1/2 cup vegetable oil
2 tablespoons dill weed
1 teaspoon lemon pepper
1/4 teaspoon garlic powder
2 (12-ounce) packages oyster crackers

Preheat the oven to 200 degrees. Combine the salad dressing mix, vegetable oil, dill weed, lemon pepper and garlic powder in a small mixing bowl. Spread the oyster crackers on a baking sheet.

Drizzle the oil mixture over the crackers. Bake for 30 minutes, stirring every 10 minutes. You can increase the amount of seasonings and salad dressing mix if desired or add crushed red pepper for a zestier flavor.

Makes 3 to 4 cups

Fall Popcorn Balls

1/4 cup (1/2 stick) butter or margarine
1 (10-ounce) package miniature marshmallows,
    about 6 cups
1 (4-ounce) package orange gelatin
12 cups popped popcorn
1 cup candy corn

Combine the butter and marshmallows in a large microwave-safe bowl. Microwave on High for 1 1/2 to 2 minutes or until the marshmallows are puffed. Stir in the gelatin.

Mix the popcorn and candy corn in a large bowl. Add the marshmallow mixture and mix to coat well. Shape into 15 balls or other desired shapes with buttered hands. Serve immediately or cool and wrap individually in plastic wrap.

Makes 12   *—From the kitchen of Young Chefs Academy*

Bill Brooks

Sergio Garcia

Dave Hermann

Loren Lee

Will Lowery

Jeff Lundy

Vicky Parker

Soren Pedersen

Richard Pignetti

Celebrated Chefs & Restaurants

When it comes to cuisine, Lone Star chefs really shine.

This great state offers many unique places to dine.

You've come to the table—sit down, be our guest.

Let us introduce you to some of Central Texas' best.

This chapter graciously underwritten by the Past Presidents of

the Junior League of Waco (see page 196)

Past Presidents of the Junior League of Waco, Inc.

1935-1936 Margaret Barclay Megarity

1936-1938 Suzanne Denise Sloane

1938-1940 Mary Buchanan McDermott

1940-1942 Edna Aynesworth Crosthwait

1942-1943 Frances Duncan Nalle

1943-1944 Mildred Chambers Sadler

1944-1945 Frances Duncan Nalle

1945-1947 Margaret Earle Buchanan

1947-1949 Helen Adelaide Mitchell

1949-1950 Alice M. Harwell

1950-1952 Frances B. Sturgis

1952-1953 Kathleen Cole Nash

1953-1954 Jane Brazelton Dudgeon

1954-1955 Pattie Rose Trippet

1955-1956 Lillian Riley Ruebeck

1956-1957 Pattie Clement Milam

1957-1958 Lucy Cox Latham

1958-1959 Marjorie Carter Lacy

1959-1960 Margaret Boyce Brown

1960-1961 Mary Ann "Koko" Lacy

1961-1962 Betty McIntosh Jackson

1962-1963 Jane Rich Scruggs

1963-1964 Billie Kay Cox

1964-1965 Jean Lewis McReynolds

1965-1966 Sue Holt Getterman

1966-1967 Roberta Hatch Bailey

1967-1968 Jean Hedrick Darden

1968-1969 Beth Miller Mayfield

1969-1970 Sarah Swift Harrison

1970-1971 Jacqueline Lake Mathias

1971-1972 Martha Dickie Dossett

1972-1973 Sandra Mayfield Coleman

1973-1974 Ann Brown Parsons

1974-1975 Cynthia Swift

1975-1976 Helen Nash Weathers

1976-1977 Sharon C. Perry

1977-1978 Barbara Martin

1978-1979 Betsy Buchanan Oates

1979-1980 Diane Varner Henderson

1980-1981 Sharon Allison

1981-1982 Sally Firmin

1982-1983 Tommye Lou Davis

1983-1984 Penny Murchison Chase

1984-1985 Teemus Warner

1985-1986 Sharon M. Fielder

1986-1987 Linda Goble Tinsley

1987-1988 Sharon Robertson

1988-1989 Alice Ogden

1989-1990 Cynthia Y. Squires

1990-1991 Paula B. Campbell

1991-1992 LuAnn A. Browder

1992-1993 Diane Jordan

1993-1994 Debbie Pence Luce

1994-1995 Jill Harvey McCall

1995-1996 Harriett Hull Fadal

1996-1997 Kathy Copeland Myatt

1997-1998 Lisa C. Jaynes

1998-1999 Cathy Dunnam Pleitz

1999-2000 Debra D. Burleson

2000-2001 Sheryl S. Swanton

2001-2002 Cheryl Allen

2002-2003 Dianne W. Sawyer

2003-2004 Rene Lyde Taylor

2004-2005 Kathy McCarty Douthit

Chicken San Marco

Pignetti's

6 boneless skinless chicken breasts
1 cup all-purpose flour
$^1\!/_4$ cup olive oil
6 tablespoons olive oil
1 medium yellow onion, sliced
12 shrimp, peeled and deveined
5 large mushrooms, sliced

$^1\!/_2$ (14-ounce) can chicken broth
$^1\!/_2$ cup heavy cream
1 cup marinara sauce
$^1\!/_4$ cup ($^1\!/_2$ stick) butter, cut into 8 pieces
salt and pepper to taste

Garnish: *grated Parmesan cheese*

Preheat the oven to 275 degrees. Coat the chicken with the flour. Heat $^1\!/_4$ cup olive oil in a large skillet and add the chicken. Sauté for 1 to 2 minutes on each side. Remove to a baking sheet and bake for 30 to 45 minutes or until cooked through.

Heat 6 tablespoons olive oil in a large skillet. Add the onion and sauté until translucent. Add the shrimp and mushrooms and sauté for 3 minutes. Stir in the chicken broth and cook until reduced by $^1\!/_2$.

Stir the cream and marinara sauce into the shrimp mixture and add the chicken. Stir in the butter 1 piece at a time and season with salt and pepper. Add additional chicken broth if necessary for the desired consistency. Garnish with Parmesan cheese to serve.

Serves 6

Richard Pignetti's culinary style is ever-evolving. He likes to create, and food is his canvas. He opened Pignetti's in Temple in 2003 as a Bistro-style Italian restaurant, serving pizzas cooked in a wood-burning oven. Trained at the Culinary Institute of America, Pignetti has received many awards. In 1998, he received an award for Best New Restaurant in Houston, and in 1999, he received the prestigious Zagat Award for Best Cuisine, Best Ambiance, and Best Service. It isn't, however, the accolades that drive him, but his passion for food.

Stacked Shrimp Enchiladas in Roasted Tomatilla Salsa

Waco's Bestyet Catering

Shrimp Stuffing
1 pound shrimp or grilled
    chicken, chopped
1/2 cup red chile paste
kosher salt and freshly ground
    pepper to taste

Enchiladas
12 crisp corn tostadas
4 cups (16 ounces) shredded
    Pepper Jack cheese
2 cups roasted tomatillo salsa
4 teaspoons (heaping) sour cream

For the shrimp stuffing, combine the shrimp, red chile paste, kosher salt and pepper to taste in a bowl and mix well.

For the enchiladas, preheat the oven to 400 degrees. Spoon 1/2 cup shrimp stuffing onto each tostada and sprinkle with 1/4 cup cheese. Stack 3 tostadas to form each serving and place the stacks on a baking sheet lined with foil.

Bake for 12 minutes or until the stuffing is bubbly. Place on serving plates and top with roasted tomatillo salsa and sour cream. Serve immediately.

Serves 4

Owned and operated by Vicky and Randall Parker, Waco's Bestyet Catering has been a part of Waco's entertainment scene since 1950. With a trademark of quality and personal pride, Vicky Parker has redefined custom catering and has been named Best Caterer by Wacoan magazine for the last three years. Parker was awarded third place in a national competition sponsored by Catersource and the International Caterers Association. Career highlights include providing food for both President George W. Bush and President George H. W. Bush.

Seared Alaskan King Crab Cakes

Waco's Bestyet Catering

> 5 tablespoons mayonnaise
> 2 tablespoons Dijon mustard
> 2 tablespoons fresh lemon juice
> 1 tablespoon Tabasco sauce
> 3 eggs
> 1 1/2 pounds king crab meat
> 3 cups (about) cracker crumbs
> 1 bunch fresh chives, chopped
> 1 cup chopped red bell pepper
> 1 or 2 teaspoons canola oil or vegetable oil

Combine the mayonnaise, Dijon mustard, lemon juice, Tabasco sauce and eggs in a large bowl and mix well. Add the crab meat, cracker crumbs, chives and bell pepper; mix gently with the hands. Shape into 20 cakes about 3/4 inch thick. Arrange on a work surface and dust lightly with flour.

Heat a sauté pan on medium-high heat and coat with the canola oil. Heat the oil and add the crab cakes a few at a time. Cook until light brown on both sides. Serve immediately with jicama slaw and dill mustard aïoli, if desired.

Serves 10

Elk Tenderloin

Diamond Back's

1/2 cup soy sauce	*1 (1-pound) elk tenderloin*
1/2 teaspoon ground thyme	
1/4 teaspoon ground nutmeg	***Garnish:*** *parsley sprigs, radish rosettes,*
1 teaspoon pepper	*sliced yellow squash*

Mix the soy sauce, thyme, nutmeg and pepper in a shallow dish. Add the elk tenderloin and marinate in the refrigerator for 8 hours or longer. Soak 1 cup of hickory chips in water for 8 hours or longer.

Preheat a grill using 5 pounds of charcoal and allowing the coals to burn for 30 minutes or preheat a gas grill for 30 minutes. Scatter the hickory chips over the coals and close the grill for 10 minutes. Drain the elk, reserving the marinade. Place the elk on the grill and baste with the reserved marinade. Grill in a closed grill for 10 minutes. Turn the elk and baste again. Grill in a closed grill for 10 minutes longer or until the elk is slightly pink in the center and still moist.

Serve with a raspberry sauce and garnish with parsley sprigs, radish rosettes and squash slices.

Serves 2 to 4

Director of Operations for International Restaurant Group, Bill Brooks has been in the restaurant business for twenty-two years, beginning with The Conrad Hilton College of Hotel and Restaurant Management in Houston. Diamond Back's features fine food with a Texas twist, and Bill includes among his career highlights cooking every year during the elk season for the guides and hunters of Flag Creek Ranch in Meeker, Colorado.

Chicken or Beef Satay

Diamond Back's

> $^1/_4$ *cup peanut oil*
> 1 *teaspoon soy sauce*
> $^1/_2$ *tablespoon honey*
> 1 *teaspoon chopped roasted garlic*
> 1 *teaspoon grated gingerroot*
> 1 *teaspoon chopped cilantro*
> 1 *teaspoon curry powder*
> $^1/_4$ *teaspoon turmeric*
> $^1/_2$ *teaspoon cumin*
> $^1/_4$ *tablespoon salt*
> $^1/_4$ *tablespoon pepper*
> $^1/_4$ *tablespoon red pepper flakes*
> 2$^1/_2$ *pounds boneless skinless chicken breasts or*
>   *beef round steak*

Combine the peanut oil, soy sauce and honey in a bowl and mix well. Add the garlic, gingerroot, cilantro, curry powder, turmeric, cumin, salt, pepper and red pepper flakes and mix well.

Slice the chicken with the grain into 3-inch strips or slice the beef across the grain into 3-inch strips. Add to the marinade and stir to coat evenly. Marinate in the refrigerator for 4 hours or longer.

Soak bamboo skewers in water. Drain the chicken or beef and thread onto the skewers. Grill until done to taste. Serve with a peanut dipping sauce made fresh from the marinade ingredients, but do not reuse the marinade. If preparing both chicken and beef satay, marinate them in separate dishes.

Serves 6

Salado Caesar Salad

Inn on the Creek

Southwestern Vinaigrette
3 large shallots, chopped
2 garlic cloves, chopped
2 jalapeño chiles, seeded and chopped
1 cup (8 ounces) plain nonfat yogurt
2 tablespoons red wine vinegar
2 tablespoons lemon juice
$1/2$ teaspoon salt
$1/4$ teaspoon coarsely ground pepper
$1/4$ cup olive oil

Salad
2 heads romaine, torn
garlic croutons
$1/4$ cup (1 ounce) freshly grated
   Parmesan cheese

For the vinaigrette, combine the shallots, garlic and jalapeño chiles in the food processor. Add the yogurt, red wine vinegar, lemon juice, salt and pepper. Process until smooth. Add the olive oil gradually, processing constantly.

For the salad, toss the lettuce with the vinaigrette in a salad bowl, coating evenly. Top with garlic croutons and the Parmesan cheese.

Serves 8 to 10

Inn on the Creek in Salado provides an elegant, yet relaxed atmosphere, making the most of seasonal vegetables and creative recipes to make the dining experience unique. The Inn has been exciting the taste buds of visitors and residents of the Village of Salado for more than eighteen years. Owner and chef Will Lowery has enjoyed cooking all his life and first began cooking for the public at community fundraisers with the previous owners of the Inn.

Savory Cheesecake

Inn on the Creek

$1/4$ cup (1 ounce) grated Parmesan cheese
1 medium onion, chopped
$1/2$ teaspoon chopped garlic
1 tablespoon bacon drippings
40 ounces cream cheese, softened
5 eggs
8 slices bacon, crisp-cooked and chopped
4 ounces blue cheese, crumbled
2 or 3 dashes of Tabasco sauce
salt and pepper to taste

Preheat the oven to 300 degrees. Sprinkle the Parmesan cheese in a buttered 10-inch springform pan.

Sauté the onion and garlic in the bacon drippings in a sauté pan until the onion is translucent. Combine the cream cheese and eggs in a food processor. Add the onion mixture, bacon, blue cheese, Tabasco sauce, salt and pepper. Process until combined with small pieces of bacon remaining.

Spoon the mixture into the prepared springform pan. Bake for $1^1/2$ hours. Turn off the oven and let the cheesecake remain in the closed oven for 1 hour. Chill for several hours before serving. Place on a plate and remove the side of the pan. Serve with fresh fruit and thinly sliced French bread.

You can omit the blue cheese and add smoked red bell pepper, Cheddar cheese and taco seasoning for a Mexican flavor, or Parmesan cheese, pesto and sun-dried tomatoes for an Italian flavor.

Serves 40

Molasses Sugar Cookies

Mirth

1 cup sugar	*2 teaspoons baking soda*
¹/4 cup molasses	*1 teaspoon cinnamon*
1 egg	*¹/2 teaspoon ginger*
³/4 cup shortening	*¹/2 teaspoon salt*
2 cups sifted all-purpose flour	

Whisk the sugar, molasses and egg together in a bowl. Melt the shortening in a medium saucepan over low heat. Add the molasses mixture and mix well. Cook until the sugar dissolves.

Sift the flour, baking soda, cinnamon, ginger and salt together. Add to the molasses mixture and mix well. Wrap in plastic wrap and chill for 3 hours.

Preheat the oven to 375 degrees. Shape the dough into 1-inch balls and roll in additional sugar. Arrange 2 inches apart on greased cookie sheets; press lightly with a fork to flatten slightly.

Bake for 8 to 10 minutes or until golden brown. Cool on wire racks to allow the cookies to firm up before removing them from the cookie sheet.

Makes 3 dozen

"Classically prepared dishes with Southern style" is the best description of Loren Lee's culinary creations. Trained at the California Culinary Academy in San Francisco, Loren is both chef and owner of Mirth, which means "happiness with laughter" and was inspired by her grandmother Muzzy. The Molasses Sugar Cookies are one of Muzzy's recipes.

Tuna Tartare

Mirth

Soy Lime Vinaigrette
1 teaspoon soy sauce
2¹/₂ teaspoons lime juice
1¹/₂ teaspoons rice wine vinegar
¹/₄ cup canola oil

Tuna
4 (4-ounce) sashimi-grade ahi tuna
   steaks, chilled
2¹/₂ teaspoons minced red onion
10 to 12 cilantro leaves, cut into
   thin strips
¹/₈ teaspoon kosher salt, or to taste

Garnish: won ton skins and canola oil

For the vinaigrette, combine the soy sauce, lime juice and vinegar in a small bowl. Whisk in the canola oil gradually. Pour into a small squeeze bottle so the mixture can be shaken at serving time if it separates.

For the tuna, cut the steaks across the grain into bite-size pieces. Combine with the onion, cilantro and salt in a bowl and toss to mix well. Add 1 or 2 tablespoons of the vinaigrette and toss to coat well. Mound in small bowls.

For the garnish, cut the won ton skins into ¹/₂-inch strips and twist the strips. Add enough canola oil to cover the strips to a saucepan or skillet. Heat the oil to 375 degrees on a candy thermometer. Add the strips and fry until golden brown and the surface begins to bubble. Remove and drain on paper towels. Sprinkle on the tuna.

Serves 4

Fillet of Beef Daniel's

The Northwood Inn

1 small onion, chopped
1 teaspoon chopped shallot
2 teaspoons chopped garlic
2 tablespoons red wine
1 teaspoon dry mustard

$1/2$ cup Jack Daniel's whiskey
10 tablespoons ($1^1/4$ sticks) butter,
   cut into 1-inch pieces
4 (6-ounce) beef fillets

Combine the onion, shallot, garlic, red wine and dry mustard in a saucepan and mix well. Cook over medium-high heat until reduced by $1/2$. Add the Jack Daniel's whiskey and ignite carefully. Let the flames subside and cook until reduced to $1/5$ of the original volume.

Reduce the heat to low and whisk in the butter 1 piece at a time. Keep warm rather than hot, as the sauce may separate at a high temperature.

Preheat the grill or broiler. Place the fillets on the grill or a rack in a broiler pan. Grill or broil until done to taste. Place 1 fillet on each serving plate and top with the Jack Daniel's sauce.

Serves 4

Jeff Lundy's specialty is continental cuisine with a southwestern flair. He has been chef and owner for eleven years of the Northwood Inn, a cottage nestled in a wooded area on Waco's north side. His previous experience includes the Skyline and Tucson Country Clubs in Arizona, as well as Waco's Brazos Club. His food is loved by Wacoans and food critics alike. He has been awarded nine medals from the American Culinary Association.

Southwestern Chicken Salad

The Northwood Inn

Cilantro Lime Vinaigrette
1/2 cup plus 2 tablespoons olive oil
1/4 cup fresh lime juice
2 tablespoons honey
2 teaspoons chopped cilantro
1 teaspoon chopped garlic

Marinated Chicken
1 cup orange juice
1/2 cup lime juice
1/4 cup lemon juice
2/3 cup tequila
1/2 small onion, chopped
1 1/2 tablespoons chopped cilantro
1 tablespoon minced garlic

2 teaspoons cumin
1 tablespoon crushed red pepper flakes
2 teaspoons salt
2 (6-ounce) skinless boneless
    chicken breasts

Salad
1 small red bell pepper, julienned
1 small green bell pepper, julienned
1/2 small red onion, julienned
2 tablespoons chopped pecans
leaves of 1 bunch spinach
1 avocado, cut into 8 wedges
1 medium tomato, cut into 8 wedges

For the vinaigrette, combine the olive oil, lime juice, honey, cilantro and garlic in a blender and process for 1 1/2 minutes or until smooth. Store in the refrigerator.

For the chicken, combine the orange juice, lime juice, lemon juice, tequila, onion, cilantro and garlic in a bowl. Stir in the cumin, red pepper flakes and salt. Add the chicken and coat well. Marinate in the refrigerator for 2 hours.

Preheat the grill. Drain the chicken and grill for 4 minutes on each side or until cooked through. Slice into strips.

For the salad, combine the chicken with the bell peppers, onion, pecans and 1/2 cup of the vinaigrette in a bowl. Place the spinach on 4 serving plates and top with the chicken mixture. Arrange the avocado and tomato on the salads and drizzle with additional vinaigrette if desired.

Serves 4

Pear and Sun-Dried Cranberry Crisp

The Range Restaurant

Crisp Topping
1 cup pecan pieces
1 cup all-purpose flour
1 cup packed light brown sugar
pinch of salt
$1/2$ cup (1 stick) unsalted butter,
    cut into small pieces

Crisp
6 tablespoons ($3/4$ stick) butter
12 pears, peeled, cored and sliced
pinch of salt
$1/2$ cup sun-dried cranberries
$1/4$ cup packed brown sugar

For the topping, combine the pecans, flour, brown sugar and salt in a bowl. Cut in the butter by hand until crumbly but still lumpy. Store in the refrigerator.

For the crisp, preheat the oven to 350 degrees. Heat the butter in a large sauté pan, but do not brown. Add the pears and salt and sweat just until the pears begin to become tender. Add the cranberries and brown sugar and cook until the brown sugar dissolves, stirring to coat the fruit evenly.

Spoon the mixture into a baking dish and sprinkle with the topping. Bake until the topping is golden brown. Serve warm or store in the refrigerator and reheat to serve.

Serves 8

American food with French and Mediterranean influences is Dave Hermann's specialty at The Range, which he opened in Salado in 1997. Dave trained at The Culinary Institute of America in Hyde Park, New York, but he claims that his greatest accomplishment has been working with his wife, Katie, to grow their business together and to achieve a good balance between their work and personal lives.

Butternut Squash Soup with Ginger Crème Fraîche

The Range Restaurant

> *5 pounds butternut squash*
> *1 bunch leeks, white portions only, chopped*
> *1/4 cup (1/2 stick) butter*
> *honey to taste*
> *ground cardamom to taste*
> *ground coriander to taste*
> *salt and pepper to taste*
> *2 quarts chicken stock*
> *heavy cream*
> *ginger crème fraîche*
>
> **Garnish:** *roasted pecans*

Preheat the oven to 350 degrees. Cut the squash into halves lengthwise and discard the seeds. Place cut side down in a baking pan and add water. Bake, covered, for 1 hour or until the squash is tender. Scoop out and reserve the pulp.

Sweat the leeks in the butter in a saucepan until tender. Add the squash and season with honey, cardamom, coriander, salt and pepper. Add the chicken stock and mix well. Simmer for 30 minutes, stirring frequently. Process the soup in batches in a blender or food processor until smooth. Strain through a china cap.

Combine the soup base with the desired amount of cream in a saucepan and bring to a boil. Ladle into bowls and drizzle with ginger crème fraîche. Garnish with roasted pecans.

You can prepare the soup base in advance and chill in the refrigerator. Add cream if needed for the desired consistency and reheat to serve.

Serves 12

Orange Pecan Cake

Ridgewood Country Club

3/4 cup pecans, toasted and cooled
1 1/3 cups all-purpose flour
1/2 cup (1 stick) butter, softened
1 cup sugar
1 tablespoon grated orange zest
1/4 teaspoon vanilla extract

1 egg
4 teaspoons baking powder
1/4 teaspoon kosher salt
1 cup milk
1/4 cup pecans, toasted and cooled

Preheat the oven to 350 degrees. Combine 3/4 cup pecans and flour in a food processor and pulse to a fine powder. Cream the butter with the sugar, orange zest and vanilla in a mixing bowl until light and fluffy.

Beat in the egg, scraping the side of the bowl. Add half the flour mixture and mix just until blended. Add the remaining flour mixture, baking powder, kosher salt and milk and mix until smooth.

Spoon into a buttered and floured 9-inch springform pan. Sprinkle with 1/4 cup pecans. Bake for 45 minutes. Cool on a wire rack. Place on a serving plate and remove the side of the pan.

Serves 8

Executive Chef Soren Pedersen's culinary style is a contemporary blend of foods from around the world, prepared simply, but with a complex play of flavor and textures. A native of Denmark, he began his training there with a four-year apprenticeship before joining Club Corp, where he worked for six years. Pedersen has been with Ridgewood Country Club since 2001. Catering to famous people, including President George Bush, Sr. and athelete Carl Lewis, are among his career highlights.

Bourbon-Cured Pork Chop with Grain Mustard Butter

Ridgewood Country Club

Grain Mustard Butter
1 pound butter, softened
2 tablespoons grain mustard
2 tablespoons Dijon mustard
3 tablespoons minced chives
1 teaspoon kosher salt
2 teaspoons ground pepper

Pork Chops
6 pork chops
10 shallots
10 garlic cloves
1 cup packed brown sugar

^{1}/4 cup vegetable oil
^{1}/4 cup bourbon
1 cup kosher salt
10 tablespoons pepper

Herb Pan Jus
reserved pork scraps
1 onion, sliced
all-purpose flour
1^1/2 cups white wine
4 cups demi-glace
1 sprig fresh thyme
1 bay leaf

For the butter, cream the butter with a paddle attachment in a mixing bowl. Add the grain mustard, Dijon mustard, chives, kosher salt and pepper and mix until smooth. Shape into a log and wrap in plastic wrap. Chill until serving time.

For the pork chops, trim the pork chops and reserve the scraps. Combine the shallots, garlic, brown sugar, vegetable oil, bourbon, kosher salt and pepper in a food processor. Pulse for 1 minute. Rub over the pork chops and let stand for 3 hours to cure.

For the pan jus, heat a saucepan until smoking. Add the reserved pork scraps and sauté until brown. Add the onion and sauté until light brown. Sprinkle with flour and add the wine, stirring to deglaze the saucepan. Add the demi-glace, thyme and bay leaf and cook until reduced by ^{1}/2. Strain and keep hot.

To finish, scrape the curing mixture off the pork chops. Grill the pork chops until cooked through. Place on serving plates. Spoon the pan jus over the pork chop and top with the butter. Serve with braised red cabbage.

Serves 6

Plato del Pacifico

El Siete Mares

1 (8-ounce) snapper fillet	1 teaspoon chopped garlic
1/4 cup fresh lime juice	3 jumbo shrimp, peeled and deveined
salt and pepper to taste	3 serrano chiles, sliced
1/4 cup (1/2 stick) butter	6 arbol chiles, chopped
1/4 cup extra-virgin olive oil	

Preheat the grill. Rub the snapper with the lime juice, salt and pepper. Grill for 6 minutes on each side. You can also bake the fish for 15 minutes or sauté until cooked through.

Melt the butter with the olive oil in a medium skillet. Add the garlic and sauté for 3 minutes. Add the shrimp and chiles and sauté for 4 minutes.

Place the fish on a serving plate and top with the shrimp and chile mixture. Serve with rice and vegetables.

Serves 1

Growing up in Vera Cruz along the Gulf side of Mexico, Sergio Garcia learned to cook fish and shellfish straight from the sea. When he came to Waco, he worked with renowned chef Geoffrey Michaels. In 1995, he opened El Siete Mares, offering seafood with a Mexican flair and using fresh ingredients and flavorful sauces. Garcia has been proud to serve people from Houston to Washington and everywhere in between, and owes his success to the people of Waco for their kind support.

Camarones à la Mexicana

El Siete Mares

Pico de Gallo
2 or 3 medium Roma tomatoes,
    seeded and chopped
1 white onion, chopped
1/2 cup chopped cilantro
2 serrano chiles, seeded and chopped
juice of 2 or 3 limes
salt to taste

Shrimp
16 to 20 extra-large shrimp
2 teaspoons Chef Geoffrey
    Michael's Spicet
2 tablespoons olive oil
1 teaspoon coarsely ground pepper

For the pico de gallo, combine the tomatoes, onion, cilantro, chiles, lime juice and salt in a bowl and mix well. Chill in the refrigerator.

For the shrimp, heat a large sauté pan over high heat for 2 minutes. Toss the shrimp with the Spicet and olive oil in a bowl. Add to the sauté pan and sauté for 1 to 2 minutes or until nearly opaque, stirring constantly.

Drain the pico de gallo and add 2 cups to the saucepan; stir in the pepper. Cook for 30 seconds longer or until the shrimp are cooked through.

Serves 2

Contributors

This book could not have been possible without the hard work and dedication of many people. The cookbook committee would like to thank the following people, who so graciously gave their favorite recipes, cooking skills, time, and support. Although we could not use all of the submitted recipes, they were outstanding. If we have inadvertently left someone out, we sincerely apologize.

Melinda Akin	Susan Bussell	Karen Deaconson	Steve Harris
Cheryl Allen	Mary Byrd	Gloria Delany	Linda Hatchel
Deann Anderson	Denise Cadell	Tracy Detchemendy	Kristen Hatton
Beth Armstrong	Ann Campbell	Carla Dever	Jennifer Heinz
Beth Arnold	Catie Capp-Hayes	Dee Dosher	Carla Hennig
Josette Ayres	Tammy Carlisle	Kathy Douthit	Erin Hesser
Kimberly Back	Bonnie Carpenter	Sarah Downs	Davina Hicks
Melle Bain	Tina Carroll	Erin Dubois	Kim Hightower
Lessie Baird	Melissa Cates	Marcie Duncan	Kathy Hillman
Lee Bankston	Margaret Cates	Rhonda Dunlap	Margaret Holland
Erin Basden	Kathy Cawthron	Michelle Dunnam	Suzanne Hollon
Pam Bell	Frances Clenegren	LaRaine DuPuy	Christy Holze
Paul Bell	Laura Clifton	Priscilla Duron	Leslie Horne
Debbie Bennett	Pat Clifton	Christine Ebbeler	Lisa Horton
Kimberley Black	Trudy Cohen	Linda Edelstein	Martha Howe
Sally Bledsoe	Judy Coker	Gretchen Eichenberg	Nancy Hoyt
Beth Boehm	Khalil Coltrain	Stephanie Evans	Susan Huey
Meredith Boozer	Leslie Coltrain	JoAn Felton	Janet Hutcheson
Tonya Bottoms	Pam Cooper	Nan Felton	Elise Hutchins
J.J. Bowling	Jan Copeland	Vivian Fisher	Laura Indergard
Lydia Bratcher	Jewell Copeland	Retha Fletcher	Loeen Irons
Gretchen Braunstein	Elizabeth Corey	Sunny Fullerton	Julie Ivey
Sylvia Bray	Sheree Corn	Tammy Gage	Beth Jablonowski
Trisha Brindley	Kay Corwin	Hilary Grant	Lisa Jaynes
Cathy Briscoe	Jan Crawford	Judy Graves	Robin Johnson
Allison Brooks	Meg Cullar	Amy Greenlee	Harriet Johnson
Jamie Brooks	Gail Cunningham	Amber Greenwood	Dana Jones
LuAnn Browder	Sharron Cutbirth	Amy Grigsby	Joyce Jones
Prissy Brown	Lucretia Darden	Betty Haas	Merryl Jones
Debra Burleson	Dave Deaconson	Missy Harris	Will Jones

Debbie Keel
Mindy Kiepke
Margaret Killian
Bill Killian
Heather Kizer
Lynn Klatt
Phyllis Koester
Carrie Kruse
Joel Kuehl
Mandy Kuehl
Linda Kuehl
Noell Lacy
Sandi Lane
Nancy Latham
Docia Lawless
Noelle LeCrone
Ellen Lee
Loren Lee
Sara Lee
Helen Lewis
Jennifer Lindsey
Debbie Luce
Lori Lutz
Frances Lynch
Po Madsen
Marie Martin
Beth Mayfield
Danni Mayfield
Denise McClinton
Guyla McClinton
Judith McCracken
Erica McKay
Jean McKinney
Teresa Mellon
Jill Michaels
Pati Milligan

John Minor
Yvonne Minor
Carol Jo Mize
Karen Mode
Ellie Morrison
Audrey Morton
Kathy Myatt
Lori Nabors
Sherry O'Connor
Alice Ogden
Bobbyee Oliver
Susie Oliver
Jessica Olson
Kris Olson
Nannette Pankenien
Becky PanKratz
Becky Parker
Amanda Parr
Cathy Pleitz
Jennifer Poe
Donna Powers
Nida Priest
Elisa Rainey
Millie Read
Susan Richards
Tammy Richards
Pat Riddle
Andrea Ridgway
Jeanette Roark
Jean Roark
Regena Rushing
Julie Ryno
Paula Sager
Dee Ann Salinas
Debbie Sartain
Dianne Sawyer

Laura Schmeltekopf
Diane Schuetze
Carol Sedberry
Traci Shamblin
Sarah Shaw
Shirley Sheffield
Jennie Sheppard
Michelle Shero
Becky Shook
Robert Shoop
Sharon Shoop
Wade Shoop
Gwynn Slavik
Janna Slechta
Charissa Sloan
Lauri Smith
Lorynn Smith
Teri Smith
Kristi SoRelle
Mandy Spikes
Melody Spivey
Cynthia Squires
Kay Standefer
Ashley Stephens
Ann Stigliano
Debbie Stock
Ricky Stock
Cindy Stovall
Jacqui Strickland
Frances Sturgis
Angie Summy
Laura Sumrall
Sheryl Swanton
Rene Taylor
Donell Teaff
Angela Tekell

Martha Therrell
Vicki Thomas
Kirsten Turner
Carla Valis
Jeanette Vandiver
Sharron Vickers
Mandy Vieregg
Michael Vieregg
Stacie Virden
Nancy Walker
Paula Wash
Leandra Wash-Cole
Lisa Watson
Natalee Watson
Ilsa Weaver
Emily White
Jolinda Whitney
Dianna Willams
Barbara Williamson
Betsy Willis
Wendy Willis
Patrice Wills
Kendra Wilson
Dawn Wilson
Lynn Wisely
Debra Witt
Robyn Wolters
Cathy Wood
Trudy Woodson
Debbie Wooley
Jamie Worley
Trey Worley
Helen Yancy
Jamie Youens
Kim Zander

Index

Accompaniments. *See also*
  Butter; Salsa; Sauces
  Candied Walnuts, 60
  Glazed Sugared Pecans, 55
  Herb Pan Jus, 211
  Pico de Gallo, 213
  Spicy Sugar, 185

Almonds
  Almond Tea, 41
  Chicken and Almond
    Salad, 62
  Mushroom Almond
    Chicken, 97
  Spring or Summer Salad, 56
  Sunflower Spinach
    Salad, 59

Appetizers. *See also* Dips; Salsa;
    Snacks; Spreads
  Bacon-Wrapped
    Chicken Bites, 22
  Blue Cheese Asparagus
    Rolls, 21
  Chicken Curry Bites, 21
  Crab Crisps, 23
  Crab Fondue, 23
  Crostini with Grilled Shrimp
    and Goat Cheese, 25
  Mini Mexican Shells, 28
  Olive and Cheese
    Crostini, 24
  Stuffed Jalapeño Chiles, 26
  Stuffed Mushrooms, 27
  Sweet Baked Brie, 20

Apple
  Apple Cake, 137
  Apple Dew Dumplings, 191
  Apple Jelly Sauce, 84
  Baked Caramel Apples, 191
  Dutch Apple Crisp, 150
  Field Greens with Apple
    and Walnuts, 180
  Heart-Warming Wassail, 45

Artichokes
  Artichoke and Rice Salad, 63
  Dilly Artichoke Cheese
    Spread, 37
  Spinach and Artichoke
    Casserole, 120

Asparagus
  Asparagus Risotto, 122
  Asparagus Vinaigrette, 112
  Blue Cheese Asparagus Rolls, 21
  Roasted Potatoes with
    Goat Cheese, 119

Avocado
  Cowboy Caviar, 30
  Salsa Verde, 35

Bacon
  Bacon-Wrapped
    Chicken Bites, 22
  Baked Eggs Benedict, 143
  Barbecued Dove, 99
  Bean Bake with Sausage, 114
  Brazos Baked Beans, 113
  Bundles of Beans, 115
  Curry Chutney Dip, 30
  Jalapeño-Stuffed Pork
    Tenderloin, 84
  Parsley and Bacon Sandwiches, 66
  Pennsylvania Dutch
    Green Beans, 115
  Savory Cheesecake, 203
  Spaghetti Carbonara, 83
  Spanish Eggs, 144
  Strawberry Salad with
    Poppy Seed Dressing, 57
  Stuffed Chicken, 183
  Stuffed Jalapeño Chiles, 26

Banana
  Banana Bread, 126
  Breakfast Slush, 42
  Oatmeal Banana Muffins, 129
  Strawberry-Banana Punch, 42

Beans
  Bean and Cheese Dip, 29
  Bean Bake with Sausage, 114
  Beans à la Chara, 113
  Black Bean and Corn Salsa, 34
  Brazos Baked Beans, 113
  Bundles of Beans, 115
  Mexican Casserole, 80
  Mexican Fiesta Salad with
    Cilantro Dressing, 53
  Pennsylvania Dutch
    Green Beans, 115
  Southwest Pot Roast, 72
  Spanish Rice, 123

Beef. *See also* Ground Beef; Veal
  Bavarian Beef, 78
  Beef Tenderloin, 73
  Carne Guisada, 71
  Chicken or Beef Satay, 201
  Dried Beef Cheese Balls, 37
  Fillet of Beef Daniel's, 206
  Greek Salad with Grilled Sirloin, 61
  Mushroom Beef Wellington, 75
  Peppercorn Tenderloin, 74
  Rolled Brisket Pot Roast, 70
  Southwest Pot Roast, 72
  Steak Santa Fe, 76
  Stuffed Chicken, 183
  Stuffed Sirloin Steak Rolls, 77
  Teriyaki Flank Steak, 182
  Three-Packet Roast, 181
  Unforgettable Beef Tips, 181

Beverages, Alcoholic
  Champagne Punch, 44
  Chocolate Martini, 45
  Freezer Milk Punch, 43
  Sangria, 44

Beverages, Nonalcoholic
  Almond Tea, 41
  Breakfast Slush, 42
  Fruity Mint Tea, 41
  Heart-Stopper Punch, 43

Heart-Warming Wassail, 45
Peppermint Hot Cocoa Mix, 179
Strawberry-Banana Punch, 42

Breads. See also Muffins
Banana Bread, 126
Bread Pudding, 154
Buttermilk Pancakes with
   Strawberry Topping, 141
Caramel French Toast, 140
Cheese Danish, 186
Cheese Petits Fours, 48
Cheese Pull-Apart Bread, 132
Cheesy Toast, 187
Cinnamon Pull-Apart Bread, 132
Focaccia, 133
Gingerbread, 138
Home-Baked Yeast Bread, 134
Honey Rolls, 135
Irish Soda Bread, 187
Lemon-Glazed Zucchini
   Pecan Bread, 127
Mexican Spoon Bread, 128
One-Hour Rolls, 136
PBJ Scones, 188
Pumpkin Bread, 126
Shellfish Crepes in
   Wine Cheese Sauce, 106
Sour Cream Coffee Cake, 139
Strawberry Nut Bread, 128

Broccoli
Broccoli Soup, 180
Crunchy Asian Slaw, 55
Sunflower Spinach Salad, 59

Butter
Cranberry Butter, 129
Grain Mustard Butter, 211

Cakes
Apple Cake, 137
Butterscotch Cake, 155
Carrot Cake, 156
Chocolate Chip Pound Cake, 189
German Chocolate
   Bundt Cake, 189
Mexican Pineapple Cake, 157
Orange Pecan Cake, 210
Rum Cake, 158
Turtle Cake, 159

Candy
Chocolate Krispies, 160
Chocolate Truffles, 160
Fabuloso Pralines, 162
Mexican Fudge, 161
Millionaire Candy, 162

Caramel
Baked Caramel Apples, 191
Caramel Dumplings, 151
Caramel Filling, 159
Caramel Sauce, 151
Chocolate Oatmeal Carmelitas, 164
Coconut Caramel Pecan Pie, 175
Millionaire Candy, 162

Carrots
Carrot Cake, 156
Healthy Morning Muffins, 131
Sweet Carrot Soufflé, 116

Cheese
Baked Eggs Benedict, 143
Bean and Cheese Dip, 29
Better Cheddar Spread, 38
Blue Cheese Asparagus Rolls, 21
Brunch Casserole, 143
Celebration Cheddar
   Cheesecake, 39
Cheese and Corn Casserole, 116
Cheese and Garlic Grits, 123
Cheese Danish, 186
Cheese Petits Fours, 48
Cheese Pull-Apart Bread, 132
Cheesy and Spicy Shrimp, 104
Cheesy Pecan Spread, 38
Cheesy Potato Casserole, 118
Cheesy Toast, 187
Chicken Fiesta, 96
Chicken Jarlsberg, 90
Chicken Tetrazzini, 95
Chicken Verde Stuffed
   Shells, 94
Corn Dip, 29
Cream Cheese Queso, 179
Crostini with Grilled Shrimp and
   Goat Cheese, 25
Dilly Artichoke Cheese
   Spread, 37
Dried Beef Cheese Balls, 37
Eggplant Parmesan, 109

Field Greens with Apple
   and Walnuts, 180
Fiesta Spread, 40
Garlic and Blue Cheese
   Mashed Potatoes, 118
Greek Salad with Grilled Sirloin, 61
Green Chile Eggs, 144
Hearty Cheese Soup, 50
Manicotti, 81
Mexican Casserole, 80
Mexican Spoon Bread, 128
Mini Mexican Shells, 28
Olive and Cheese Crostini, 24
Parmesan Chicken Breasts, 92
Pumpkin Tureen, 31
Queso Flameado, 33
Roasted Potatoes with
   Goat Cheese, 119
Savory Cheesecake, 203
Shellfish Crepes in
   Wine Cheese Sauce, 106
Sour Cream Chicken Enchiladas, 87
Spaghetti Pie, 185
Spicy Vegetable Garden
   Chowder, 52
Stacked Shrimp Enchiladas in
   Roasted Tomatilla Salsa, 198
Stuffed Red Peppers, 117
Stuffed Shells, 182
Sweet Baked Brie, 20
Swiss Cheese Spread, 178
Tailgate Sandwiches, 67
Texas Chowder, 49
Tomato Basil Soup, 48
Wine Cheese Sauce, 107

Cheesecakes
Celebration Cheddar
   Cheesecake, 39
Savory Cheesecake, 203

Chefs
Brooks, Bill, 194, 200
Garcia, Sergio, 194, 212
Hermann, Dave, 194, 208
Lee, Loren, 194, 204
Lowery, Will, 194, 202
Lundy, Jeff, 194, 206
Parker, Vicky, 194, 198
Pedersen, Soren, 194, 210
Pignetti, Richard, 194, 197

Chicken
- Bacon-Wrapped Chicken Bites, 22
- Champagne Chicken with Shrimp, 89
- Cheesy Chicken and Cabbage Soup, 50
- Chicken and Almond Salad, 62
- Chicken Casserole with Rice and Vegetables, 93
- Chicken Curry Bites, 21
- Chicken Fiesta, 96
- Chicken Italian, 90
- Chicken Jarlsberg, 90
- Chicken or Beef Satay, 201
- Chicken Pie, 91
- Chicken Pot Pie, 184
- Chicken Salad Sandwich Supreme, 66
- Chicken San Marco, 197
- Chicken Tetrazzini, 95
- Chicken Verde Stuffed Shells, 94
- Gourmet Chicken Spaghetti, 88
- Green Chile Chicken Casserole, 184
- Mushroom Almond Chicken, 97
- Parmesan Chicken Breasts, 92
- Poppy Seed Chicken Casserole, 92
- Sour Cream Chicken Enchiladas, 87
- Southwestern Chicken Salad, 207
- Stuffed Chicken, 183
- Sweet-and-Sour Chicken, 183

Chiles/Peppers
- Barbecued Dove, 99
- Black Bean and Corn Salsa, 34
- Carne Guisada, 71
- Cheese and Corn Casserole, 116
- Chicken Fiesta, 96
- Chipotle Peach Sauce, 20
- Cilantro Dressing, 53
- Corn Dip, 29
- Cowboy Caviar, 30
- Creamy Hominy Casserole, 117
- Green Chile Chicken Casserole, 184
- Green Chile Eggs, 144
- Jalapeño-Stuffed Pork Tenderloin, 84
- Mexican Spoon Bread, 128
- Pico de Gallo, 35, 213
- Plato del Pacifico, 212
- Red Pepper and Garlic Shrimp, 107
- Salsa Verde, 35

- Sausage Bundles, 142
- Shrimp with Grits and Roasted Peppers, 105
- South of the Border Salsa, 34
- Southwestern Vinaigrette, 202
- Stacked Shrimp Enchiladas in Roasted Tomatilla Salsa, 198
- Steak Santa Fe, 76
- Stuffed Jalapeño Chiles, 26
- Stuffed Red Peppers, 117

Chocolate
- Brazos Brownies, 163
- Brownie Frosting, 163
- Brownie Pie, 171
- Chocolate Chip Pound Cake, 189
- Chocolate Frosting, 159
- Chocolate Ganache, 148
- Chocolate Krispies, 160
- Chocolate Martini, 45
- Chocolate Mint Ice Cream, 152
- Chocolate Oatmeal Carmelitas, 164
- Chocolate Pie, 171
- Chocolate Toffee Ice Cream Bar Dessert, 153
- Chocolate Truffles, 160
- Fudge Sauce, 153
- German Chocolate Bundt Cake, 189
- Heart-Stopper Punch, 43
- Hot Fudge Sauce, 192
- Kahlúa Bars, 166
- Layered Dessert Bars, 170
- Mexican Fudge, 161
- Milky Way Ice Cream, 152
- Millionaire Candy, 162
- Mocha Velvet Torte, 148
- Peanut Butter Oatmeal Cookies with Chocolate Chips, 165
- Peppermint Hot Cocoa Mix, 179
- Pots de Crème, 149
- Turtle Cake, 159
- White Chocolate Macadamia Cookies, 167

Coconut
- Carrot Cake, 156
- Coconut Caramel Pecan Pie, 175
- Coconut Cream Pie, 172
- Coconut Meringue, 172
- Layered Dessert Bars, 170

Coffee
- Heart-Stopper Punch, 43
- Kahlúa Bars, 166
- Kahlúa Frosting, 166
- Mexican Fudge, 161
- Mocha Velvet Torte, 148

Cookies
- Brazos Brownies, 163
- Chocolate Oatmeal Carmelitas, 164
- Christmas Fruit Drop Cookies, 168
- Jubilee Jumbles, 169
- Kahlúa Bars, 166
- Layered Dessert Bars, 170
- Molasses Sugar Cookies, 204
- Peanut Butter Oatmeal Cookies with Chocolate Chips, 165
- Pecan Bars, 190
- Rosemary Cookies, 170
- Toffee Bars, 190
- White Chocolate Macadamia Cookies, 167

Corn
- Black Bean and Corn Salsa, 34
- Cheese and Corn Casserole, 116
- Corn Dip, 29
- Mexican Spoon Bread, 128
- Polka-Dot Potatoes and Beef, 79

Crab Meat
- Crab Cakes, 103
- Crab Crisps, 23
- Crab Fondue, 23
- Seared Alaskan King Crab Cakes, 199
- Shellfish Crepes in Wine Cheese Sauce, 106

Cranberry
- Chicken Curry Bites, 21
- Cranberry Butter, 129
- Fall or Winter Salad, 56
- Frozen Cranberry Salad, 64
- Heart-Warming Wassail, 45
- Pear and Sun-Dried Cranberry Crisp, 208
- Spinach Salad with Pecan Vinaigrette, 58
- Tangy Cranberry Orange Muffins, 130

Desserts. *See also* Cakes; Candy; Cookies; Ice Cream; Pies, Sweet
Apple Dew Dumplings, 191
Baked Caramel Apples, 191
Bread Pudding, 154
Caramel Dumplings, 151
Chocolate Toffee Ice Cream Bar Dessert, 153
Crème Brûlée, 149
Crème de Menthe Parfaits, 151
Dutch Apple Crisp, 150
Mocha Velvet Torte, 148
Peach Cobbler, 150
Pear and Sun-Dried Cranberry Crisp, 208
Pots de Crème, 149
Strawberries Romanoff, 192

Dips. *See also* Salsa
Bean and Cheese Dip, 29
Corn Dip, 29
Cowboy Caviar, 30
Cream Cheese Queso, 179
Curry Chutney Dip, 30
Heart of Texas Shrimp Dip, 36
Picadillo, 32
Pico de Gallo, 35
Pumpkin Tureen, 31
Queso Flameado, 33
Shrimp and Salsa, 36
Sweet Cream Dip, 178

Egg Dishes
Baked Eggs Benedict, 143
Breakfast Pizza, 142
Brunch Casserole, 143
Green Chile Eggs, 144
Spanish Eggs, 144

Enchiladas
Sour Cream Chicken Enchiladas, 87
Stacked Shrimp Enchiladas in Roasted Tomatilla Salsa, 198

Fish. *See also* Salmon; Tuna
Plato del Pacifico, 212

Frostings
Brownie Frosting, 163
Chocolate Frosting, 159
Cream Cheese Frosting, 157
Kahlúa Frosting, 166

Fruit. *See also* Apple; Avocado; Banana; Coconut; Cranberry; Grape; Lemon; Lime; Orange; Peach; Pear; Pineapple; Raspberry; Strawberry
Christmas Fruit Drop Cookies, 168
Frozen Fruit Salad, 65
Healthy Morning Muffins, 131
Sangria, 44

Game/Game Birds
Barbecued Dove, 99
Elk Tenderloin, 200
Quail in Mushroom Sauce, 101

Glazes
Browned Butter Glaze, 169
Brown Sugar Glaze, 137
Cream Cheese Glaze, 132
Honey Glaze, 135
Lemon Glaze, 127
Orange Glaze, 130
Rum Glaze, 158
Turkey Glaze, 98

Grape
Cornish Game Hens, 100
Grape Salad, 64

Grits/Hominy
Cheese and Garlic Grits, 123
Creamy Hominy Casserole, 117
Shrimp with Grits and Roasted Peppers, 105

Ground Beef
Beef and Vegetable Stew, 51
Homemade Spaghetti Sauce, 82
Manicotti, 81
Mexican Casserole, 80
Mini Mexican Shells, 28
Picadillo, 32
Polka-Dot Potatoes and Beef, 79
Stuffed Shells, 182

Ham/Prosciutto
Asparagus Risotto, 122
Celebration Cheddar Cheesecake, 39
Tailgate Sandwiches, 67

Ice Cream
Chocolate Mint Ice Cream, 152
Chocolate Toffee Ice Cream Bar Dessert, 153
Milky Way Ice Cream, 152

Junior League History
Art of Learning, The, 100
Bookworms, 51
CAPP, 165
Children's Advocacy Center, 122
First Fundraisers, 22
Getting Creative, 62
Getting Together for Kids, 96
Going Wild, 112
Granting Community Wishes, 192
Great Discoveries, 178
Having A Ball, 40
Helping Hospitals, 71
Heritage Square, 153
Historic Waco Foundation, 39
Hoopin' It Up, 139
It's Showtime, 86
Kids Kastle, 72
LEAPS, 188
Let's Play, 95
Making Beautiful Music Together, 74
Pot of Gold, A, 140
Safety Comes First, 161
School Supply Train, 155
Shop 'Til You Drop, 31
Showing Compassion, 173
Show on a String, 109
Waco Children's Symphony, 24
When Disaster Strikes, 33
Women in Wartime, 26
World of Color, A, 174

Lemon
Lemon Glaze, 127
Lemon-Glazed Zucchini Pecan Bread, 127
Lemon Sauce, 108

Lime
Cilantro and Lime Rice, 121
Cilantro Lime Vinaigrette, 207
Key Lime Pie, 173

Muffins
Healthy Morning Muffins, 131
Oatmeal Banana Muffins, 129
Tangy Cranberry Orange
Muffins, 130

Mushrooms
Mushroom Almond
Chicken, 97
Mushroom Beef Wellington, 75
Mushroom Empanadas, 145
Mushroom Stuffing, 97
Peppered Mushroom Sauce, 73
Quail in Mushroom Sauce, 101
Roasted Mushroom Salad, 54
Shallot and Mushroom-Stuffed
Turkey Breasts with
Madeira Sauce, 98
Spanish Eggs, 144
Steak Santa Fe, 76
Stuffed Mushrooms, 27
Three-Packet Roast, 181

Nuts. *See* Almonds; Pecans; Walnuts

Orange
Heart-Warming Wassail, 45
Orange Glaze, 130
Orange Pecan Cake, 210
Sunflower Spinach Salad, 59
Tangy Cranberry Orange
Muffins, 130

Pasta
Bavarian Beef, 78
Champagne Chicken with
Shrimp, 89
Chicken Tetrazzini, 95
Chicken Verde Stuffed
Shells, 94
Gourmet Chicken Spaghetti, 88
Manicotti, 81
Pasta with Scallops, 103
Spaghetti Carbonara, 83
Spaghetti Pie, 185
Stuffed Shells, 182

Pastry/Pie Shell
Chicken Pie Pastry, 91
Cream Cheese Pastry, 145
Graham Cracker Pie Shell, 173

Peach
Chipotle Peach Sauce, 20
Peach Cobbler, 150

Peanut Butter
Chocolate Krispies, 160
PBJ Scones, 188
Peanut Butter Oatmeal Cookies
with Chocolate Chips, 165

Pear
Butter Lettuce Salad with
Pomegranate Vinaigrette, 60
Pear and Sun-Dried Cranberry
Crisp, 208

Pecans
Apple Cake, 137
Better Cheddar Spread, 38
Cheesy Pecan Spread, 38
Chocolate Krispies, 160
Christmas Fruit Drop
Cookies, 168
Coconut Caramel
Pecan Pie, 175
Crisp Topping, 208
Crunchy Asian Slaw, 55
Fabuloso Pralines, 162
Fall or Winter Salad, 56
Fiesta Spread, 40
Frozen Cranberry Salad, 64
Glazed Sugared Pecans, 55
Layered Dessert Bars, 170
Lemon-Glazed Zucchini
Pecan Bread, 127
Mexican Pineapple
Cake, 157
Millionaire Candy, 162
Mystery Pecan Pie, 174
Orange Pecan Cake, 210
Pecan Bars, 190
Pecan Topping, 121
Pecan Vinaigrette, 58
Rum Cake, 158
Strawberry Salad with
Poppy Seed Dressing, 57

Pies, Savory
Chicken Pie, 91
Chicken Pot Pie, 184
Spaghetti Pie, 185

Pies, Sweet
Brownie Pie, 171
Chocolate Pie, 171
Coconut Caramel
Pecan Pie, 175
Coconut Cream Pie, 172
Key Lime Pie, 173
Mystery Pecan Pie, 174
Strawberry Pie, 175

Pineapple
Apple Jelly Sauce, 84
Baked Pineapple, 186
Breakfast Slush, 42
Carrot Cake, 156
Champagne Punch, 44
Frozen Cranberry Salad, 64
Fruity Mint Tea, 41
Mexican Pineapple Cake, 157

Pork. *See also* Bacon; Ham/Prosciutto;
Sausage
Bourbon-Cured Pork Chop with
Grain Mustard Butter, 211
Jalapeño-Stuffed Pork
Tenderloin, 84
Marinated Pork Tenderloin, 85
Sour Cream Pork Chops, 86

Potatoes. *See also* Sweet Potatoes
Breakfast Pizza, 142
Cheesy Potato Casserole, 118
Garlic and Blue Cheese
Mashed Potatoes, 118
Polka-Dot Potatoes and
Beef, 79
Roasted Potatoes with
Goat Cheese, 119

Poultry. *See also* Chicken;
Game/Game Birds; Turkey
Cornish Game Hens, 100

Pumpkin
Pumpkin Bread, 126
Pumpkin Tureen, 31

Raspberry
Raspberry Coulis, 148
Raspberry Mustard Sauce, 85
Raspberry Poppy Seed Dressing, 56

Restaurants
Diamond Back's, 200, 201
El Siete Mares, 212, 213
Inn on the Creek, 202, 203
Mirth, 204, 205
Northwood Inn, The, 206, 207
Pignetti's, 197
Range Restaurant, The, 208, 209
Ridgewood Country Club, 210, 211
Waco's Bestyet Catering, 198, 199

Rice
Artichoke and Rice Salad, 63
Asparagus Risotto, 122
Chicken Casserole with
    Rice and Vegetables, 93
Cilantro and Lime Rice, 121
Mushroom Almond Chicken, 97
Spanish Rice, 123
Wild Rice and Tuna Salad, 63

Salad Dressings
Balsamic Vinaigrette, 54
Basil Vinaigrette, 61
Cilantro Dressing, 53
Cilantro Lime Vinaigrette, 207
Maple Balsamic Vinaigrette, 180
Pecan Vinaigrette, 58
Pomegranate Vinaigrette, 60
Poppy Seed Dressing, 57
Raspberry Poppy Seed
    Dressing, 56
Sandwich Dressing, 67
Slaw Dressing, 55
Southwestern Vinaigrette, 202
Soy Lime Vinaigrette, 205
Sweet-and-Sour Vinaigrette, 59

Salads
Artichoke and Rice Salad, 63
Asparagus Vinaigrette, 112
Butter Lettuce Salad with
    Pomegranate Vinaigrette, 60
Chicken and Almond Salad, 62
Chicken Salad Sandwich
    Supreme, 66

Crunchy Asian Slaw, 55
Fall or Winter Salad, 56
Field Greens with Apple
    and Walnuts, 180
Frozen Cranberry Salad, 64
Frozen Fruit Salad, 65
Grape Salad, 64
Greek Salad with
    Grilled Sirloin, 61
Mexican Fiesta Salad with
    Cilantro Dressing, 53
Roasted Mushroom Salad, 54
Salado Caesar Salad, 202
Seasonal Salads with Raspberry
    Poppy Seed Dressing, 56
Southwestern Chicken Salad, 207
Spinach Salad with
    Pecan Vinaigrette, 58
Spring or Summer Salad, 56
Strawberry Salad with
    Poppy Seed Dressing, 57
Sunflower Spinach Salad, 59
Wild Rice and Tuna Salad, 63

Salmon
Cajun Salmon, 101
Cedar Plank Salmon with
    Potlatch Seasoning, 102

Salsa
Black Bean and Corn Salsa, 34
Salsa Verde, 35
Shrimp and Salsa, 36
South of the Border Salsa, 34

Sandwiches
Chicken Salad Sandwich
    Supreme, 66
Parsley and Bacon Sandwiches, 66
Tailgate Sandwiches, 67

Sauces, Savory
Apple Jelly Sauce, 84
Chipotle Peach Sauce, 20
Coca-Cola ® Barbecue Sauce, 99
Homemade Spaghetti Sauce, 82
Lemon Sauce, 108
Madeira Sauce, 98
Peppered Mushroom Sauce, 73
Raspberry Mustard Sauce, 85
Wine Cheese Sauce, 107

Sauces, Dessert
Caramel Sauce, 151
Chocolate Ganache, 148
Fudge Sauce, 153
Hot Fudge Sauce, 192
Raspberry Coulis, 148
Whipped Cream Sauce, 138
Whiskey Sauce, 154

Sausage
Bean Bake with Sausage, 114
Breakfast Pizza, 142
Brunch Casserole, 143
Cream Cheese Queso, 179
Homemade Spaghetti
    Sauce, 82
Sausage Bundles, 142
Spaghetti Carbonara, 83
Spicy Vegetable Garden
    Chowder, 52
Stuffed Mushrooms, 27
Stuffed Sirloin Steak Rolls, 77
Texas Chowder, 49

Seafood. See also Crab Meat;
    Fish; Shrimp
Pasta with Scallops, 103

Shrimp
Camarones à la Mexicana, 213
Champagne Chicken with
    Shrimp, 89
Cheesy and Spicy Shrimp, 104
Chicken San Marco, 197
Crostini with Grilled Shrimp
    and Goat Cheese, 25
Heart of Texas
    Shrimp Dip, 36
Plato del Pacifico, 212
Red Pepper and
    Garlic Shrimp, 107
Shellfish Crepes in
    Wine Cheese Sauce, 106
Shrimp and Salsa, 36
Shrimp Creole, 104
Shrimp Gumbo, 49
Shrimp Stuffing, 198
Shrimp with Grits and
    Roasted Peppers, 105
Stacked Shrimp Enchiladas in
    Roasted Tomatilla Salsa, 198

Snacks
Fall Popcorn Balls, 193
Oyster Crackers, 193

Soups
Beef and Vegetable Stew, 51
Broccoli Soup, 180
Butternut Squash Soup with
    Ginger Crème Fraîche, 209
Cheesy Chicken and
    Cabbage Soup, 50
Hearty Cheese Soup, 50
Shrimp Gumbo, 49
Spicy Vegetable Garden Chowder, 52
Texas Chowder, 49
Tomato Basil Soup, 48

Spinach
Brunch Casserole, 143
Chicken Verde Stuffed Shells, 94
Seasonal Salads with Raspberry
    Poppy Seed Dressing, 56
Southwestern Chicken Salad, 207
Spinach and Artichoke
    Casserole, 120
Spinach Salad with
    Pecan Vinaigrette, 58
Sunflower Spinach Salad, 59

Spreads
Better Cheddar Spread, 38
Celebration Cheddar Cheesecake, 39
Cheesy Pecan Spread, 38
Cranberry Butter, 129
Dilly Artichoke Cheese Spread, 37
Dried Beef Cheese Balls, 37
Fiesta Spread, 40
Swiss Cheese Spread, 178

Squash
Butternut Squash Soup with
    Ginger Crème Fraîche, 209
Garden Squash Casserole, 120

Strawberry
Better Cheddar Spread, 38
Champagne Punch, 44
Spring or Summer Salad, 56
Strawberries Romanoff, 192
Strawberry-Banana Punch, 42
Strawberry Nut Bread, 128
Strawberry Pie, 175
Strawberry Salad with
    Poppy Seed Dressing, 57
Strawberry Topping, 141

Stuffings
Mushroom Stuffing, 97
Shrimp Stuffing, 198

Sweet Potatoes
Southern Sweet Potatoes, 121
Spicy Sweet Potato Wedges, 185

Toffee
Chocolate Toffee Ice Cream Bar
    Dessert, 153
Layered Dessert Bars, 170
Toffee Bars, 190

Tomatoes
Pico de Gallo, 35, 213
Salsa Verde, 35
South of the Border Salsa, 34
Spanish Eggs, 144
Stuffed Red Peppers, 117
Tomato Basil Soup, 48

Toppings
Crisp Topping, 208
Pecan Pie Topping, 174
Pecan Topping, 121
Strawberry Topping, 141

Tortillas
Mexican Casserole, 80
Sour Cream Chicken Enchiladas, 87

Tuna
Tuna Tartare, 205
Wild Rice and Tuna Salad, 63

Turkey
Breakfast Pizza, 142
Shallot and Mushroom-Stuffed
    Turkey Breasts with Madeira
    Sauce, 98
Tailgate Sandwiches, 67

Veal Scallops in Lemon Sauce, 108

Vegetables. *See also* Artichokes;
    Asparagus; Beans; Broccoli;
    Carrots; Chiles/Peppers; Corn;
    Mushrooms; Potatoes; Pumpkin;
    Spinach; Squash; Tomatoes;
    Zucchini
Beef and Vegetable Stew, 51
Cheesy Chicken and
    Cabbage Soup, 50
Chicken Casserole with
    Rice and Vegetables, 93
Chicken Pie, 91
Chicken Pot Pie, 184
Cowboy Caviar, 30
Eggplant Parmesan, 109
Picadillo, 32
Spicy Vegetable Garden
    Chowder, 52

Walnuts
Candied Walnuts, 60
Carrot Cake, 156
Field Greens with Apple
    and Walnuts, 180
Healthy Morning Muffins, 131

Zucchini
Chicken Jarlsberg, 90
Lemon-Glazed Zucchini
    Pecan Bread, 127

Simply Serving

Recipes from the Heart of Texas

Junior League of Waco, Inc.
2600 Austin Avenue • Waco, Texas 76710 • "Cookbook Order"
254-753-5574

Name _____

Address _____

City _____ State _____ Zip _____

Telephone _____ Email _____

Please send me _____ copies of *Simply Serving* at $24.95 each $ _____

Texas residents add 8.25% sales tax $ _____

Postage and handling at $5.50 for one book and
$1.50 for each additional book shipped to same address $ _____

Gift wrapping at $2.00 per book $ _____

TOTAL $ _____

Method of Payment: [   ] MasterCard   [   ] VISA
[   ] Check or money order payable to the Junior League of Waco

Account Number _____ Expiration Date _____

Signature _____

By purchasing this book, you are supporting the community projects
of the Junior League of Waco and making an investment in the lives of many.

Photocopies will be accepted.